PANORAMA

BUILDING PERSPECTIVE THROUGH LISTENING

2

DAPHNE MACKEY

LAURIE BLASS

ELLEN KISSLINGER

with HELEN HUNTLEY, MARY MARCH,
and ANASTASSIA TZOYTZOYRAKOS

OXFORD
UNIVERSITY PRESS

OXFORD
UNIVERSITY PRESS

198 Madison Avenue
New York, NY 10016 USA

Great Clarendon Street, Oxford OX2 6DP UK

Oxford University Press is a department of the University of Oxford.
It furthers the University's objective of excellence in research, scholarship,
and education by publishing worldwide in

Oxford New York

Auckland Cape Town Dar es Salaam Hong Kong Karachi
Kuala Lumpur Madrid Melbourne Mexico City Nairobi
New Delhi Shanghai Taipei Toronto

With offices in

Argentina Austria Brazil Chile Czech Republic France Greece
Guatemala Hungary Italy Japan Poland Portugal Singapore
South Korea Switzerland Thailand Turkey Ukraine Vietnam

OXFORD and OXFORD ENGLISH are registered trademarks of
Oxford University Press.

© Oxford University Press 2007

Database right Oxford University Press (maker)

Developer: Angela M. Castro, English Language Trainers
Editorial Director: Sally Yagan
Publishing Manager: Pietro Alongi
Editor: Rob Freire
Associate Editor: Beverley Langevine
Design Director: Robert Carangelo
Senior Designer: Michael Steinhofer
Art Editor: Robin Fadool
Production Manager: Shanta Persaud
Production Controller: Soniya Kulkarni

STUDENT BOOK ISBN: 978 0 19 475707 2
PACK ISBN: 978 0 19 475713 3

Printed in Hong Kong

10 9 8 7 6 5 4 3 2 1

Acknowledgments:

Cover art:
Hans Hofmann
Combinable Wall I and II
1961
Oil on canvas
Overall: 84-1/2 x 112-1/2 inches
University of California, Berkeley Art Museum: Gift of the artist.

The publisher would like to thank the following for their permission to
reproduce photographs: © Liz Boyd/Alamy, v; © Martin Harvey/Alamy, 1;
Illustrated by Woodshed, 2; © Bobby Model/National Geographic Collection/
Getty Images, 2; © David Wall/Alamy, 5; © imagebroker/Alamy, 8; © Michel
Arnaud/CORBIS, 13; © nicorien/Nico le Roux, 14; © Brand X Pictures/Alamy,
17; © Craig Lovell/Eagle Visions Photography/Alamy, 17; © PATRICK LIN/
Stringer/AFP/Getty Images, 20; © VIEW Pictures Ltd/Alamy, 25; © Arcaid/
Alamy, 26; © Kim Karpeles/Alamy, 26; COURTESY NASA, 29; © Alejandro
Castro/Castro Designs, 32; © Rajesh Jantilal/PANAPRESS/Getty Images, 37;
© FETHI BELAID/Stringer/AFP/Getty Images, 38; © AFP/Getty Images, 41;
© ATTILA KISBENEDEK/Staff/AFP/Getty Images, 44; © Travel Ink Photo
Library/ Index Stock Imagery, 49; © Bettmann/CORBIS, 50; © Bettmann/
CORBIS, 53; © Index Stock Imagery, 56; © Stone/Getty Images, 61; © Pictorial
Press Ltd./Alamy, 62; © Pictorial Press Ltd./Alamy, 62; © International Spy
Museum, 65; © Courtesy Everett Collection, 68; © Photo Japan/Alamy, 73;
© Christie's Images/CORBIS, 74; © Jon Arnold Images/Alamy 77; © Digital
Vision/Getty Images, 80; © Justin Guariglia/National Geographic/ Getty
Images, 80; © Content Mine International/Alamy, 85; © Steve Nichols/Alamy,
85; Courtesy wikipedia.org/wiki/Image, 86; © Hulton Archive/Stringer/Getty
Images, 89; © ImageState/Alamy, 92.

The authors and publisher would like to acknowledge the following
individuals for their invaluable input during the development of this series:
Russell Frank, Pasadena City College, CA; Maydell Jenks, Katy Independent
School District, TX; Maggie Saba, King Abdulaziz University in Jeddah, Saudi
Arabia; Grant Trew, Oxford University Press, Japan; Heidi Vande Voort Nam,
Department of English Education, Chongshin University, Seoul, South Korea.

CONTENTS

TO THE TEACHER

Welcome to *Panorama Listening 2,* a listening skills book for high-beginning level students. *Panorama Listening 2* combines high-interest listening passages from the content areas with a strong vocabulary strand and extensive listening skills practice to prepare students for the challenges of academic listening.

As in the companion reading strand, each of the eight main units in *Panorama Listening* consists of three chapters, and each chapter has a thematically-linked listening passage. The first passage is about a person, the second on a related place, and the third on a related concept or event. The topics in each unit are related to those in the corresponding unit of *Panorama Reading*.

The book begins with an introductory unit, **Essential Listening Skills**, that presents and practices the basic listening skills needed for academic success.

WHAT IS IN EACH UNIT?

Before You Listen
This opening page introduces the theme of the unit. The questions and photographs can be used to activate students' prior knowledge and stimulate discussion before listening.

Prepare to Listen
This section introduces the topic of the chapter. The questions and photographs encourage students to become engaged in the topic while sharing their own thoughts and experiences.

Word Focus 1
This activity introduces students to new or unfamiliar words that they will hear in the listening passage. Students match the words with simple definitions.

Make a Prediction
This activity encourages students to make a prediction about a specific piece of information that appears in the listening passage. The aim is to motivate students to listen to the passage to find the answer.

Listening Passage
Each listening in Book 2 is about 500 words. The language is carefully graded so that students gain confidence in listening.

Check Your Comprehension
These multiple-choice and true/false questions check students' understanding of the passage. The questions include key skills such as understanding the main idea, listening for details, and listening for inference.

Word Focus 2
In this activity students are introduced to 10 target vocabulary items related to the topic of the chapter in the context of a reading passage. Students have already heard these words in the listening passage. After reading the passage, students match the words with definitions. These vocabulary items will be useful for the discussion activity that follows.

Discuss the Theme
In this section of the chapter students are given the opportunity to discuss questions related to the topic of the chapter and the information they learned from the reading and listening passage.

Vocabulary Review
This section reviews the vocabulary presented in the unit. It includes a wide variety of activities, such as **Words in Context** (filling in the gaps), **Wrong Word** (finding the word that doesn't fit the group), and **Word Families** (choosing the part of speech that fits). These activities help students use the new words as part of their active vocabulary.

Wrap It Up
This final section of the unit gives students the opportunity to extend the knowledge they have acquired from the listening and reading passage and their discussions to the world outside the classroom.

For the **Project Work** students are asked to conduct a survey, prepare a presentation, or attend presentations. This can be done individually, in pairs, or in small groups.

For the **Internet Research** students are asked to research a topic related to the listening passage. This activity integrates a number of skills and encourages students to work independently.

The **Essential Listening Skills: Answer Key and Explanations**, a **Vocabulary Index**, and a list of **Common Irregular Verbs** can be found at the back of the book for easy reference.

The *Audio Scripts, Answer Key,* and eight *Unit Tests* are available in the *Answer Key and Test Booklet* that accompanies *Panorama Listening 2.*

ESSENTIAL LISTENING SKILLS

A ROBOT IN EVERY HOME

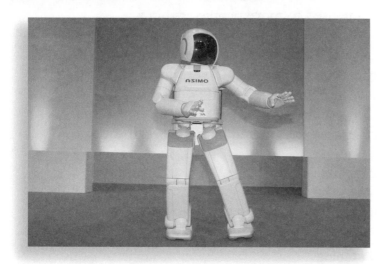

Asimo, a humanoid robot

PREVIEW AND PREDICT

Before you listen, preview and predict. When you preview, you look at the title, pictures, vocabulary, and questions. When you predict, you make logical guesses about content.

A. Look at the picture only. (Don't read the caption yet.) Answer these questions.

1. Describe what you see. _____

_____

2. What things can you guess or predict about the content of the listening passage from the picture? _____

_____

B. Now read the title and caption. Answer these questions.

1. What information does the title tell you? _____

2. What information does the caption tell you? _____

3. Do you think robots always look like this one? _____

4. What do you think *humanoid* means? _____

✔ Look at page 97 for the explanations.

C. Now preview the vocabulary.

1. This passage is probably going to describe robots. What words do you expect to hear? Make a list and share it with a classmate.

2. Now look at the list of words below. You will hear these words in the listening passage. Were any of your words in this list?

   elevator - a machine in a building used to move people or things from one floor to another

   pets - animals that you keep in your home for company or pleasure

   refrigerator - a piece of electrical equipment used to keep food cold

   robot - a machine that can move and that can be made to do some of the work that a person does

   seal - a gray animal with short fur that lives in and near the ocean and that eats fish

   trays - flat pieces of plastic or metal, etc. with raised edges that you can use to carry food, drinks, etc.

   vacuum - clean by using a machine that sucks up dirt

D. Make a prediction about the listening.

Robots are used in businesses.

a. True   **b.** False

🎧 **Now listen to the news report on robots. Check your prediction.**

✔ Look at page 97 for the explanations.

WHAT TO DO WHILE YOU LISTEN

MAIN IDEA

Every listening passage has a main idea. This is the most important topic or most general idea. Preview the main idea question below.

E. 🎧 Now listen to the lecture again. Identify the main idea in question 1. Circle your answer.

MAIN IDEA
1. What is the main topic?
   A. Robots are popular toys.
   B. We will all have robots in the future.
   C. The first robots were used in companies.
   D. Robots have many different forms and uses.

✔ Look at page 97 for the explanation.

DETAIL

Every passage has many smaller, specific pieces of information that tell you more about the main idea. These are called details. Read the questions below.

F. 🎧 **Listen to the audio again and answer the questions. Circle your answers.**

DETAIL

2. What is planned in Korea and Japan?
   A. Everyone will have a robot by 2015.
   B. Everyone will have a robot by 2050.
   C. Every home will have a robot by 2015.
   D. Every home will have a robot by 2050.

3. Robotic toys
   A. are pets
   B. are for adults
   C. have sensors
   D. want people to respond to them

4. Which of the following is **not** true?
   A. A social robot interacts with people.
   B. A social robot has sensors to recognize voices.
   C. A social robot does work that people often do.
   D. A social robot is designed to keep adults company.

5. Almost a million people own robots that clean the floor.
   A. True
   B. False

6. Robots in office buildings do **not**
   A. vacuum
   B. write letters
   C. keep watch for fire and robberies
   D. welcome people and answer questions

7. A humanoid robot is different because it
   A. can talk
   B. can clean the house
   C. can respond to people
   D. has a head, body, and legs

8. At the moment, humanoid robots
   A. keep older people company
   B. can do anything that people do
   C. cost too much to be very common
   D. can serve people food and drinks in hospitals

✔ Look at page 98 for the explanations.

G. Listen to the passage and answer the questions. Circle your answers.

INFERENCE

9. You have to train a social robot to
   A. move
   B. use sensors
   C. make sounds
   D. recognize voice commands

10. In the future, which of these will probably be true?
    A. Robots will be bigger.
    B. Robots will be less expensive.
    C. Robots will have feelings just like humans.
    D. all of the above

 Look at page 99 for the explanations.

WORDS IN CONTEXT, PART 1

H. Circle the answers with the same meaning as the words in boldface. Then underline the clues that helped you.

1. They move and make noises when you touch them, so they seem to **respond** to you.
   A. express or feel doubt about something
   B. say or do something as an answer or a reaction to something
   C. have pieces of equipment that can find certain sounds, movements, etc.

2. Designers are making **social** robots for adults, especially for older people who may not be able to get out and see other people a lot.
   A. of a high quality
   B. connected with how good something is for everyone
   C. connected with meeting people and enjoying yourself

3. These robots **interact** with their owners and keep them company.
   A. try to make somebody do something
   B. communicate or mix in a way that has an influence or effect on somebody else
   C. use force to move or try to move somebody or something forward or away from you

WORDS IN CONTEXT, PART 2

Sometimes the speaker gives a clue by defining the words while speaking. The speaker might include a definition, for example, or a synonym.

4. Underline the part of the sentence that helps define *sensors*.

They can do this because they have **sensors** that find and recognize different kinds of information.

5. Underline an example of the word *command*.

You give it a **command**. For example, you can tell it to clean the floor.

6. Underline the definition of the word *humanoid*.

But the most interesting robots are **humanoid** robots—robots that look like people.

✔ Look at page 99 for the explanations.

ANTHROPOLOGY
THE SAHARA

Crossing the Sahara Desert on camels

BEFORE YOU LISTEN

Answer these questions.

1. Where is the Sahara Desert?

2. What do you know about the Sahara?

3. Do you think the Sahara would be a good place to travel to? Why or why not?

CHAPTER 1
THE TUAREG PEOPLE

North Africa ▶

◀ Tuareg man

PREPARE TO LISTEN

Look at the map and picture above. Discuss these questions.

1. What do you think life is like in the Sahara Desert?

2. Describe the man in the picture. Why do you think he is dressed the way he is?

WORD FOCUS 1

Match the words with their definitions.

ancestors	dye	nomadic	traders
anthropologist	herders	tent	veils

1. the people in a family who lived a long time ago _____
2. pieces of material to cover the face _____
3. moving from place to place _____
4. a substance used to change the color of cloth _____
5. a scientist who studies other cultures _____
6. people who take care of animals such as sheep or goats _____
7. people who buy and sell things _____
8. a shelter made of cloth _____

MAKE A PREDICTION

The Tuareg people live in one place for a long time.

a. True   **b.** False

🎧 **Now listen to a radio interview about the Tuareg. Check your prediction.**

🎧 **Listen to the audio again and answer the questions. Circle your answers.**

MAIN IDEA

1. What is the main topic?
   A. Tuareg clothes
   B. Tuareg men
   C. Tuareg life
   D. Tuareg jobs

DETAIL

2. Which is **not** a country where the Tuareg live?
   A. Kenya
   B. Libya
   C. Burkina Faso
   D. Mali

3. The Berbers were from southwest Africa.
   A. True
   B. False

4. Why are the Tuareg called the "Blue People"?
   A. They like the blue sky of the desert.
   B. The color blue means sad and unhappy.
   C. The dye in their clothes colors their skin.
   D. Their tents are blue.

5. Which statement about veils is true?
   A. Veils protect Tuareg men from hot tea.
   B. Veils protect the face from wind and sun.
   C. Tuareg men don't wear veils at home.
   D. All Tuareg women and children wear veils.

6. Tuareg women own their family's tent.
   A. True
   B. False

7. Which of these is an occupation for the Tuareg today?
   A. trading
   B. making jewelry
   C. tour guide
   D. all of the above

8. Why don't the Tuareg build houses in the desert?
   A. The Tuareg are nomads.
   B. The Tuareg don't like houses.
   C. The Tuareg like the city better.
   D. The Tuareg don't spend much time in the desert.

INFERENCE

9. The traditional way the Tuareg travel in the desert is
   A. in buses
   B. on horses
   C. on camels
   D. in jeeps

10. What will you probably find in a Tuareg tent?
    A. blue clothing
    B. a lot of furniture
    C. a large refrigerator
    D. all of the above

Read this e-mail about the radio interview. Notice the bold words. Then match the bold words to their definitions below.

To: KXRO Radio
Subject: your report about the Tuareg people

I was **fortunate** to hear your report about the Tuareg. My ancestors from Portugal were a little like the Tuareg. Their **culture** was different. But their **experiences** were similar. They made their living as herders and farmers. Their homes were in small villages **located** in the country. Over the years, my ancestors moved to the cities so they could get good jobs. They gave up their **traditional** way of life. They took other **occupations**.

To me, the Tuareg people **symbolize** the past. The **identity** of the Tuareg people comes from the desert. They ride on camels, live in **temporary** villages, and wear traditional clothing. I think the Tuareg have to **protect** their traditional way of life. Or they will lose something very important.

A.

1. culture ___
2. experiences ___
3. fortunate ___
4. identity ___
5. located ___

a. the things that you have done
b. found in a particular place
c. who or what a person is
d. lucky
e. the customs and ideas of a particular group

B.

1. occupations ___
2. protect ___
3. symbolize ___
4. temporary ___
5. traditional ___

a. represent an idea
b. jobs or professions
c. keep something safe
d. connected with customs or beliefs from the past
e. lasting for a short time; not permanent

DISCUSS THE THEME

Read these questions and discuss them with a partner.

1. Imagine a day with the Tuareg. What would the day include?

2. Which is better in the desert, a camel or a jeep? Why?

CHAPTER 2
LIFE IN THE DESERT

The market near
the Mud Mosque

PREPARE TO LISTEN

Look at the picture above. Discuss these questions.

1. Describe the picture.
2. What do you think makes this place unique?

WORD FOCUS 1

Match the words with their definitions.

abandoned	dates back to	hippos	mud
artisans	dunes	landscapes	

1. soft, wet earth _____
2. has existed since _____
3. very large mammals that live in African rivers _____
4. local artists _____
5. no longer used _____
6. low hills of sand in a desert _____
7. views across an area of land _____

MAKE A PREDICTION

Mali is mentioned as a tourist destination.

a. True   **b.** False

🎧 **Now listen to a radio advertisement. Check your prediction.**

CHECK YOUR COMPREHENSION

 Listen to the audio again and answer the questions. Circle your answers.

MAIN IDEA

1. What is the main topic?
   A. You can buy interesting gifts in the markets in Mali.
   B. There are many things to do in Mali.
   C. You have to ride a camel to experience the Sahara Desert.
   D. The Niger River flows through Mali.

DETAIL

2. How big is the Sahara Desert?
   A. 30,000 sq. miles (77,700 sq. kilometers)
   B. 500,000 sq. miles (1,295,000 sq. kilometers)
   C. 3,500,000 sq. miles (9,065,000 sq. kilometers)
   D. 13,500,000 sq. miles (34,965,000 sq. kilometers)

3. Mali has
   A. beautiful landscapes
   B. interesting history
   C. varied cultures
   D. all of the above

4. How long is the basic trip?
   A. 3 days
   B. 8 days
   C. 10 days
   D. 24 days

5. What is one thing the travelers will **not** do in Bamako?
   A. prepare for a trip down the Niger River
   B. visit the artisans' village
   C. attend a traditional dance
   D. visit a market

6. The Grand Mosque is located in Bamako.
   A. True
   B. False

7. Which town or city is a busy port?
   A. Timbuktu
   B. Djenné
   C. Djenné-Jeno
   D. Mpoti

8. What will travelers do on the three-day trip?
   A. visit the villages of the Dogon people
   B. spend three more days on the Niger River
   C. ride a camel
   D. learn to make leather bags

INFERENCE

9. Why is the tour called an "adventure" tour?
   A. The travelers will do exciting and unusual things.
   B. The travelers will stay in big hotels.
   C. The travelers will eat in expensive restaurants.
   D. all of the above

10. People who sign up for a trip like this
    A. like to be comfortable
    B. like to save money
    C. like to travel to different, unusual places
    D. like to stay in one place on a vacation

Read this e-mail response to the radio advertisement. Notice the bold words. Then match the bold words to their definitions below.

To: Adventure Tours
Subject: Your Mali tour

I heard your advertisement about the **adventure** tour to Mali. I never thought about Mali as a travel **option**. However, after I heard about so many **unique** and **varied** places to visit there, I'll consider traveling to Mali.

I would like to recommend another country in North Africa as your next **destination**: Morocco. Five years ago, I taught English in Morocco. I stayed for two years, so I know this **fascinating** country well. Why do I think you should offer a tour to Morocco? Well, first, the **hospitality** of the Moroccan people is amazing. People were so friendly. Also, like Mali, Morocco has desert landscapes and interesting cities. In Marrakech, I tried delicious food and met people from all over. In Fez, I visited ancient **structures**. There are also **remote** villages, the Atlas Mountains, and excellent beaches. Morocco has a **complex** culture. It's a mix of Arab, Berber, and French culture. It's a great place to travel. I hope you plan a tour there.

A.
1. adventure ___   **a.** a place where someone is going
2. complex ___   **b.** being friendly and helpful to guests
3. destination ___   **c.** very interesting
4. fascinating ___   **d.** difficult to understand
5. hospitality ___   **e.** an experience that is very unusual or exciting

B.
1. option ___   **a.** different from each other
2. remote ___   **b.** far away from where other people live
3. structures ___   **c.** a thing that you can choose
4. unique ___   **d.** not like anything else
5. varied ___   **e.** buildings

Read these questions and discuss them with a partner. Share your ideas with the class.

1. Would you like to go on an adventure vacation? Where would you go?

2. Which country would you prefer to visit, Mali or Morocco? Why?

CHAPTER 3
SAHARAN ROCK ART

Rock art in the
Sahara Desert

PREPARE TO LISTEN

Look at the picture above. Discuss these questions.

1. Have you ever seen ancient rock art? Where was it?
2. Why do you think ancient people drew on rocks?

WORD FOCUS 1

Match the words with their definitions.

archeologists	carvings	clues
canyons	caves	theft

1. taking something that belongs to someone else _____
2. large holes in the side of a mountain or under the ground _____
3. people who study objects from ancient civilizations _____
4. pieces of information that help you answer a question _____
5. deep valleys with very steep sides _____
6. drawings or designs cut in stone or wood _____

MAKE A PREDICTION

Most rock art is found in places where few people live.

a. True   **b.** False

🎧 **Now listen to part of a lecture. Check your prediction.**

Listen to the audio again and answer the questions. Circle your answers.

MAIN IDEA

1. What is the main topic?
   A. Some animals that lived in the Sahara are now gone.
   B. Humans like to make drawings.
   C. Rock art is very old.
   D. Rock art gives us clues to ancient people's lives.

DETAIL

2. The climate of the Sahara has always been hot and dry.
   A. True
   B. False

3. Which of the following is **not** a kind of rock art?
   A. a photo of camels
   B. a painting of a horse
   C. a drawing of a rhinoceros
   D. a carving of a design

4. The oldest rock art in the Sahara may be
   A. 100 years old
   B. 10,000 years old
   C. 100,000 years old
   D. 1,000,000 years old

5. According to the passage, what animals were important?
   A. dogs
   B. cats
   C. cattle
   D. birds

6. Which is **not** a name for a period of Saharan rock art?
   A. Horse Period
   B. Cattle Period
   C. Buffalo Period
   D. Rhinoceros Period

7. How many examples of Saharan rock art are there?
   A. over 3,000
   B. over 13,000
   C. over 30,000
   D. over 300,000

8. Why can we still find rock art?
   A. Most rock art is found in areas where people live.
   B. Much of the rock art is protected in caves and canyons.
   C. People never stole or damaged the rock art.
   D. The climate of the Sahara was once very wet.

INFERENCE

9. Why do we see certain animals in rock art?
   A. The animals were common in the area.
   B. Some of the animals were hunted.
   C. The people needed the animals to live.
   D. all of the above

10. What is the biggest problem with rock art today?
    A. finding rock art
    B. understanding rock art
    C. keeping people from hurting rock art
    D. none of the above

Read this student's summary of the lecture. Notice the bold words. Then match the bold words to their definitions below.

> A lot of rock art **exists** in the Sahara Desert. Ancient people **created** it thousands of years ago. It **covers** the period from about 2,000 to 10,000 years ago. There are four periods of Saharan rock art. The names of the periods are: Buffalo, Cattle, Horse, and Camel. For example, the Buffalo Period **ranges** from about 8,000 to 6,000 years ago. Rock art gives **evidence** that humans lived in the Sahara Desert during that time.
>
> You can **search** for rock art in caves and canyons. The location helped **preserve** the rock art. However, people now know where the rock art is. Archeologists want to **prevent** **damage** and theft, but it's hard to control such a **vast** area.

A.

1. covers ___
2. created ___
3. damage ___
4. evidence ___
5. exists ___

a. is real; is found
b. includes
c. information that gives a reason to believe something
d. harm something
e. caused something new to happen

B.

1. preserve ___
2. prevent ___
3. ranges ___
4. search ___
5. vast ___

a. stretches from one thing to another, within certain limits
b. stop something from happening
c. extremely big
d. look for something carefully
e. keep something safe or in good condition

DISCUSS THE THEME

Read these questions and discuss them with a partner. Share your ideas with the class.

1. What do you think people can do to preserve rock art?

2. Should tourists be allowed to visit the rock art? Why or why not?

VOCABULARY REVIEW

Fill in the blanks with words from each box.

evidence	fortunate	option	temporary

1. Rock art gives _____ of the way people lived thousands of years ago.
2. The nomadic Tuareg travel around the Sahara. They live in _____ villages.
3. You have the _____ of going to Mali or Morocco.
4. We were _____ to hear the lecture about the Dogon people.

damage	destination	remote	vast

5. Mali has become a tourist _____ for many people.
6. The Sahara Desert is almost as _____ as the United States.
7. We were in the most _____ area of the country. It was far from any cities.
8. The wind can cause serious _____ to ancient structures.

WRONG WORD

One word in each group does not fit. Circle the word.

1. painting   drawing   fascinating   carving
2. canyon   ancestor   landscape   dune
3. abandoned   amazing   spectacular   unique
4. covers   ranges   includes   searches
5. occupations   jobs   professions   clues
6. identities   tents   houses   structures

WORD FAMILIES

Fill in the blanks with words from each box.

| tradition (*noun*) | traditional (*adjective*) | traditionally (*adverb*) |

1. You can see _____ dancing in Mali.
2. It is a _____ for Tuareg men to wear blue clothing.
3. _____, many North Africans were farmers or herders.

| creation (*noun*) | creative (*adjective*) | create (*verb*) |

4. Tuareg jewelry is an artistic _____.
5. The tour company wants to _____ an exciting trip to Morocco.
6. The people who drew the rock art were very _____.

WRAP IT UP

PROJECT WORK

With a partner, prepare a presentation on a place you would like to visit. It can be anywhere in the world, but not a big city. In your presentation, answer these questions:

- Where is the place?
- What is the best time of year to visit? (Consider weather, holidays, festivals, etc.)
- What can you do there? (Include places to visit, foods, shopping, etc.)
- Why do you want to go there?

Print a map and pictures, if you can. Present your information to the class.

INTERNET RESEARCH

Go online and find information about a culture in a North African country. Find answers to questions such as:

- What are some unique things about the culture?
- How is life changing in the 21st century for these people?
- What are the people doing to keep their traditions?

Print a photo of people from that country, if you can. Present your information to the class.

BUSINESS
THE FASHION INDUSTRY

▲
Fashion models

BEFORE YOU LISTEN

Answer these questions.

1. Do you like the clothing in this picture? Why or why not?

2. How much do you care about fashion?

3. Where do you buy most of your clothes?

CHAPTER 1
ANDRE KIM: FASHION DESIGNER

◀ Andre Kim (in white)
at a fashion show

PREPARE TO LISTEN

Look at the picture above. Discuss these questions.

1. Where are these people? What are they wearing?
2. What does a fashion designer do?

WORD FOCUS 1

Match the words with their definitions.

awards	models	style	top
high fashion	salon	tailors	

1. people whose job is to make clothes, usually by hand _____
2. people whose job is to wear clothing at a fashion show _____
3. prizes for doing something well _____
4. best; highest _____
5. the fashion, shape, or design of something _____
6. the finest clothing _____
7. a clothing store for high fashion _____

MAKE A PREDICTION

Andre Kim only became successful in the last ten years.

a. True   **b.** False

🎧 **Now listen to a news report on Andre Kim. Check your prediction.**

Listen to the audio again and answer the questions. Circle your answers.

MAIN IDEA

1. What is the main topic?
   A. Andre Kim is South Korea's top fashion designer.
   B. South Korea is becoming a fashion center.
   C. Andre Kim dresses in a unique way.
   D. There are now many good Korean fashion designers.

DETAIL

2. Which of the following was true when Andre Kim started his career?
   A. Tailors made clothes for Koreans.
   B. French clothing designers were popular.
   C. There was little interest in high fashion in Korea.
   D. all of the above

3. When was Andre Kim born?
   A. 1935
   B. 1945
   C. 1955
   D. 1965

4. A lot of men were fashion designers in Korea.
   A. True
   B. False

5. Why did Andre Kim change his name?
   A. He didn't like his real French name.
   B. His real name was difficult to remember.
   C. French names were connected with fashion.
   D. The name Andre made him seem older.

6. Which of the following is **not** true?
   A. Andre Kim dresses in an unusual way.
   B. Andre Kim sold his clothes in his own store.
   C. Andre Kim worked very hard to become successful.
   D. Andre Kim had a fashion show in France when he was 27.

7. According to the passage, Andre Kim's fashion shows
   A. are only in Paris
   B. use only famous fashion models
   C. are art experiences
   D. are a way for opera singers to become famous

8. Andre Kim has
   A. won awards for his paintings
   B. worked as a fashion model around the world
   C. been a very successful actor
   D. brought Korean fashion and art to the world

INFERENCE

9. What makes Andre Kim different from other designers?
   A. He only designs white clothes.
   B. He has a fashion salon.
   C. His designs show Korean traditions.
   D. He gets up very early and reads a lot.

10. What is probably true about South Korea today?
    A. There are no tailors in South Korea today.
    B. Most Korean clothing comes from France.
    C. There is more interest in designer clothing.
    D. Everyone wears Andre Kim's fashions.

Read this e-mail about the news report. Notice the bold words. Then match the bold words to their definitions below.

To: WNFQ Radio
Subject: Andre Kim

My son wants to be a **fashion designer**. But other kids **criticize** and make fun of him. So he was happy to hear about Andre Kim. Andre Kim **focused** on his dream. He didn't pay attention to what other people said. At that time South Korean **manufacturers** weren't making high fashion clothing. He didn't **imitate** French designers. His designs have their own **look**. He made South Korea famous for fashion. His strong **work ethic** helped him do well.

It's interesting that Kim thinks of a fashion show as a **performance**. I wish I could see one! It's great that he gives money from his shows to **charity**. Andre Kim really sounds like a good man. I hope that my son will work hard like Andre Kim.

A.

1. charity ___   **a.** say what is bad or wrong with someone
2. criticize ___   **b.** style of dressing; clothing
3. designer ___   **c.** gave all one's attention to something
4. fashion ___   **d.** an organization that collects money to help people who are poor or sick
5. focused ___   **e.** a person whose job is to make drawings and show how something should be made

B.

1. imitate ___   **a.** a fashion or style
2. look ___   **b.** the right way to work; hard work
3. manufacturers ___   **c.** something that you do to entertain people
4. performance ___   **d.** companies that make things
5. work ethic ___   **e.** copy something

DISCUSS THE THEME

Read these questions and discuss them with a partner.

1. Do you think fashion is art? Why or why not?

2. What are some differences between "high fashion" and what you buy?

CHAPTER 2
MILAN

Milan, Italy

Italian sportscars

PREPARE TO LISTEN

Look at the pictures above. Discuss these questions.

1. What are some things Italy is famous for?
2. Do you own anything that was made in Italy? What?

WORD FOCUS 1

Match the words with their definitions.

bargain	shops	warehouse stores
mall	sidewalk	

1. a large building that has many types of stores _____
2. small stores, usually with just one type of product _____
3. very large stores that sell things at low cost _____
4. surface on the side of a street where people can walk _____
5. something that is cheap or at a lower price than usual _____

MAKE A PREDICTION

Milan is famous for fashion.

a. True   **b.** False

🎧 **Now listen to this radio ad and conversation. Check your prediction.**

Listen to the audio again and answer the questions. Circle your answers.

MAIN IDEA

1. What is the main topic?
   A. Milan has a lot of designers.
   B. Milan is an interesting place to visit.
   C. The man likes to spend a lot of money.
   D. The man and woman are shopping for a car.

DETAIL

2. Milan has a lot of big warehouse stores.
   A. True
   B. False

3. The man bought a designer suit
   A. at a shop in Milan
   B. from a man on the sidewalk
   C. designed by Gucci
   D. from a discount store

4. Which word means the same as *handbag*?
   A. praise
   B. pursue
   C. purse
   D. press

5. Which of the following is **not** true?
   A. The man likes to shop.
   B. The man likes cars.
   C. The man suggests a trip to New York.
   D. The woman wants to go to Paris and Milan.

6. The man likes opera.
   A. True
   B. False

7. The man does **not** know
   A. Milan is in Italy
   B. Milan is in the northern part of Italy
   C. the names of Italian car companies
   D. where he bought the handbag

8. The man and woman decide to go to Paris instead.
   A. True
   B. False

INFERENCE

9. Which of the following is probably true?
   A. The woman will tell the man to buy a car in Italy.
   B. The woman is interested in visiting museums.
   C. The man spends a lot of money on clothes.
   D. The man thinks the woman will spend more money in Italy.

10. They will visit
    A. Hong Kong
    B. Milan
    C. New York
    D. all of the above

Read this review of a trip to Milan from a travel website. Notice the bold words. Then match the bold words to their definitions below.

> I just got back from a trip to Milan. Everything was **perfect**! We stayed at a hotel close to all the shops. We could look out our window and see the old buildings all lit up at night. The **architecture** is amazing.
>
> We took a bus tour one day. The country outside Milan is very **scenic**. The driver took us to a **local** mall where they had designer handbags at a **discount**. They were so cheap that we thought they were **counterfeit**. The driver promised us that they weren't fake. Most were $100, but they were **worth** more. What **a find**!
>
> On the way back, the bus drove us through an area where a lot of the **wealthy** people live. That was interesting to see, too. The houses were beautiful. Milan won't **replace** Rome as the Italian city everyone thinks of first. But it was a great place to visit.

A.

1. architecture ___   **a.** a thing that you buy that is unusually good or valuable
2. counterfeit ___   **b.** the style or design of buildings
3. discount ___   **c.** of or near a particular place
4. a find ___   **d.** copied so it looks like the real thing
5. local ___   **e.** a lower price than usual

B.

1. perfect ___   **a.** having a lot of money; rich
2. replace ___   **b.** as good as it can be
3. scenic ___   **c.** having a particular value, in money
4. wealthy ___   **d.** take the place of something
5. worth ___   **e.** having a beautiful view

DISCUSS THE THEME

Read these questions and discuss them with a partner. Share your ideas with the class.

1. How do you find good prices? Do you shop at discount stores? Or do you look for sales at regular stores?

2. Have you ever bought a handbag or watch on the street? Was it real or counterfeit? How can you tell?

CHAPTER 3
DESIGNER BRANDS

Shopping for designer handbags

PREPARE TO LISTEN

Look at the picture above. Discuss these questions.

1. Name some products by famous designers. How do you know who the designer is?

2. What are some other things famous designers sell?

WORD FOCUS 1

Match the words with their definitions.

brands	lifestyle	luggage
label	logo	perfumes

1. the way you live _____
2. company names used to identify products _____
3. a company name written on a product _____
4. a symbol used as an advertisement by a company _____
5. good-smelling liquids, used on the body _____
6. bags and suitcases for traveling _____

MAKE A PREDICTION

Fashion designers are trying to sell more than clothes.

a. True   **b.** False

🎧 **Now listen to a lecture on designer brands. Check your prediction.**

Listen to the audio again and answer the questions. Circle your answers.

MAIN IDEA

1. What is the main topic?
   A. designer clothing
   B. lifestyle brands
   C. image and fashion
   D. Ralph Lauren and Armani

DETAIL

2. Which of the following describes a lifestyle brand?
   A. common and boring
   B. inexpensive
   C. good taste
   D. all of the above

3. Which of these lifestyle products is **not** mentioned?
   A. perfumes
   B. furniture
   C. make-up
   D. linens

4. A lifestyle brand creates a positive feeling.
   A. True
   B. False

5. Why does the speaker discuss Ralph Lauren?
   A. Ralph Lauren is the best fashion designer.
   B. Ralph Lauren is her friend.
   C. The company has good taste.
   D. It's a good example.

6. Only fashion companies can have lifestyle brands.
   A. True
   B. False

7. Which way of showing a brand is mentioned?
   A. logos
   B. colors
   C. fabrics
   D. all of the above

8. Which of the following is probably true?
   A. Not all products can be lifestyle products.
   B. Everyone wants to buy expensive lifestyle brands.
   C. Companies aren't interested in lifestyle brands.
   D. Fashion designers like to design washing machines.

INFERENCE

9. People who buy lifestyle brands
   A. don't spend a lot of money
   B. want to show their good taste to others
   C. never buy things over the Internet
   D. none of the above

10. Which of these is an example of a lifestyle product?
    A. a scarf with the price on it
    B. luggage from a discount store
    C. a watch with the designer's logo
    D. sunglasses from the drugstore

Read this student's e-mail to a classmate. Notice the bold words. Then match the bold words to their definitions below.

Today in class we talked about lifestyle brands. People get **positive** feelings about brands. Then the companies **branch out** and put their names on other kinds of **products**. The companies go into different **industries**. For example, the fashion company Armani sells lamps and tables.

Is the professor saying that this is a good idea? I guess it's good for the companies. They make more money, right? It's **natural** to want to make money.

I wouldn't pay more for a product that has a designer label. I choose products because of my own **taste**, not because of the **image** the brand **represents**. I don't need my clothing or my furniture to be **associated with** a designer. Of course, I'm a student, so I don't have the money to buy **luxury** items.

A.
1. associated with ___
2. branch out ___
3. image ___
4. industries ___
5. luxury ___

a. types of manufacturing
b. something that is enjoyable and expensive but not needed
c. the feeling that a company gives to people
d. start to do new and different things
e. connected with

B.
1. natural ___
2. positive ___
3. products ___
4. represents ___
5. taste ___

a. good
b. stands for; is a symbol of
c. usual or normal; what you expect
d. a liking for something
e. the things that companies make or sell

DISCUSS THE THEME

Read these questions and discuss them with a partner. Share your ideas with the class.

1. Do you buy designer brands or lifestyle brands? Why or why not?

2. What other companies have branched out and sell different types of products under their brand name?

VOCABULARY REVIEW

WORDS IN CONTEXT

Fill in the blanks with words from each box.

charity	fashions	industry	performance

1. Members of the fashion _____ hold a special show every year.
2. They have a special _____ and invite all their best customers to watch.
3. These wealthy guests want to buy the newest _____ at the show.
4. After the show, the designers give all the money to _____.

counterfeit	fakes	luxury	manufacturers

5. A lot of people want to buy _____ items such as designer handbags.
6. Some _____ produce almost exact copies of these popular items.
7. They sell these _____ products at a cheaper price than the originals.
8. These _____ are a big problem for the designers who made the original handbags.

WRONG WORD

One word in each group does not fit. Circle the word.

1. salon   shop   mall   sidewalk
2. counterfeit designer   fake   imitation
3. discount   expensive   exclusive   wealthy
4. brand   label   logo   natural
5. opera   image   performance   show
6. award   designer   manufacturer   tailor

WORD FAMILIES

Fill in the blanks with words from each box.

| performer *(noun)* | performance *(noun)* | perform *(verb)* |

1. The _____ includes music, dance, and video.
2. Only one _____ in the show is famous. The others are unknown.
3. They _____ in two shows every Saturday.

| criticism *(noun)* | critical *(adjective)* | criticize *(verb)* |

4. At first, people were very _____ of her new designs.
5. They used to _____ her choice of colors and materials.
6. Later, her designs became popular with the public. Everyone forgot their earlier _____ of her work.

WRAP IT UP

PROJECT WORK

Survey four people outside of class about fashion. Ask them the following questions:

- How much do you like to shop?
- What is your favorite place to shop? Why?
- What's most important to you—the label, design, price, or something else?

Present your findings to the class. Discuss the results with your classmates.

INTERNET RESEARCH

Go online and find information about a new or famous fashion designer. Find answers to the following questions:

- How did this person get a start in the fashion industry?
- What is this person known for?
- Where can you find this designer's clothes? Does this designer have a lifestyle brand?

Print a photo of the designer's clothes, if you can. Present your information to the class.

ARCHITECTURE
PUBLIC SPACES

The Milwaukee Art Museum, Wisconsin, USA;
Design by Santiago Calatrava

BEFORE YOU LISTEN

Answer these questions.

1. Describe the building in the picture.

2. What do you find most interesting about that building?

3. Can a building be a work of art? Give reasons.

CHAPTER 1
SANTIAGO CALATRAVA: ARCHITECT

Santiago Calatrava, 1951–

The Lyon Airport Station, France; Design by Santiago Calatrava

PREPARE TO LISTEN

Look at the pictures above. Discuss these questions.

1. Would you have Calatrava design a house for you? Why or why not?

2. What does this building look like?

WORD FOCUS 1

Match the words with their definitions.

dramatic	knights	structure	time capsule
graceful	multi-talented	take off	

1. exciting; something that creates a big effect _____
2. a building or parts of something built _____
3. having many skills _____
4. a box to be opened in the future, filled with objects from the present _____
5. start flying _____
6. soldiers who fought on horses for the king _____
7. having beauty and elegance _____

MAKE A PREDICTION

Santiago Calatrava is also a painter.

a. True   **b.** False

🎧 **Now listen to a presentation by two student architects. Check your prediction.**

CHECK YOUR COMPREHENSION

🎧 **Listen to the audio again and answer the questions. Circle your answers.**

MAIN IDEA

1. What is the main topic?
   A. design and construction of buildings
   B. Santiago Calatrava's bridges
   C. the life and work of a great architect
   D. the art of Santiago Calatrava

DETAIL

2. When was Santiago Calatrava born?
   A. in 1921
   B. in 1928
   C. in 1951
   D. in 1958

3. Santiago Calatrava was born in beautiful Venice, Italy.
   A. True
   B. False

4. How old was Calatrava when he went to France to study?
   A. 8
   B. 13
   C. 18
   D. 28

5. Calatrava has a Ph.D. in civil engineering.
   A. True
   B. False

6. What is unique about the Lyon Airport Station?
   A. It looks like a bird.
   B. It has photos of birds.
   C. It is colorful.
   D. all of the above

7. Which of the following is true about Santiago Calatrava?
   A. He spends all of his time in museums.
   B. Each of his buildings is named after an animal.
   C. His buildings often look like his art.
   D. He studied birds when he was in France.

8. Santiago Calatrava designed the Metropolitan Museum of Art.
   A. True
   B. False

INFERENCE

9. What is true about Calatrava?
   A. He lived away from his parents.
   B. His ancestors were from France.
   C. He couldn't afford to go to college.
   D. His father was a knight.

10. Why does Calatrava talk about the language of geometry?
    A. He failed that course in school.
    B. He wanted to learn to read math problems.
    C. He likes the beauty of geometric forms.
    D. He thinks people should study foreign languages.

Read the following e-mail response to the presentation. Notice the bold words. Then match the bold words to their definitions below.

To: Lisa and Mark
Subject: Your presentation

I think that your **presentation** about Santiago Calatrava was very interesting. I agree with you about the **value** of a really great **design** in architecture.

My favorite Calatrava building is called the "Turning Torso." It's an apartment building in Sweden. It's 623 feet (190 meters) high. Can you guess from its name what this building looks like? It looks like a person turning his body or torso. This is the most unique thing about this structure.

Just like you **mentioned** in your presentation, you can see Calatrava's **background** as an artist. His designs for buildings often look like his art. *The Turning Torso* was one of his sculptures. One of the builders of a new housing project in Sweden saw this sculpture. The builder **admired** the design. He asked Calatrava to use the same **concepts** to design the apartment building. Calatrava agreed and **construction** started. People admired this amazing structure. It won several awards.

I hope that someday I can be in a **competition** with Calatrava. His work **certainly** is unique.

A.
1. admired ___
2. background ___
3. certainly ___
4. competition ___
5. concepts ___

a. education and experience
b. definitely; for sure
c. an organized event in which people try to win
d. ideas
e. respected or liked very much

B.
1. construction ___
2. design ___
3. mentioned ___
4. presentation ___
5. value ___

a. a plan or drawing showing how something will be built
b. talked about something
c. a talk that gives information on a subject
d. the usefulness or importance of something
e. the act or method of building something

DISCUSS THE THEME

Read these questions and discuss them with a partner.

1. What multi-talented people do you know? What are their talents?

2. Do you have any special talents? What are they?

CHAPTER 2
KANSAI INTERNATIONAL AIRPORT

A satellite view of Kansai International Airport, Japan

PREPARE TO LISTEN

Look at the picture above. Discuss these questions.

1. What is interesting about the airport in the picture?
2. What ways have you traveled? Which is your favorite?

WORD FOCUS 1

Match the words with their definitions.

artificial island	earthquakes	pleasure	typhoons
board	facilities	survive	

1. sudden violent movements of the earth's surface _____
2. get on a plane _____
3. places in a building for special activities _____
4. continue to exist _____
5. an island made by people, not natural _____
6. dangerous ocean storms with very strong winds _____
7. enjoyment rather than work _____

MAKE A PREDICTION

Kansai International Airport was built in two years.

a. True   **b.** False

🎧 **Now listen to an interview for a local newspaper. Check your prediction.**

Listen to the audio again and answer the questions. Circle your answers.

MAIN IDEA

1. What is the main topic?
   A. sightseeing in Osaka, Japan
   B. Kansai Airport's artificial island
   C. impressions of the Kansai region
   D. the Kansai Airport

DETAIL

2. Why does the passenger have plenty of time for the interview?
   A. His plane isn't leaving yet.
   B. He missed his plane.
   C. His plane is boarding.
   D. His flight was cancelled.

3. What kind of project is the man working on?
   A. a new airport
   B. an office building
   C. a new house
   D. none of the above

4. Which of the following is true?
   A. The man knows very little about the airport.
   B. The man was one of the architects for the airport.
   C. The man is a tourist on vacation.
   D. none of the above

5. What place did the man visit?
   A. a hotel on an island
   B. a school
   C. a famous castle
   D. an art museum

6. Renzo Piano was the main architect for the Kansai Airport.
   A. True
   B. False

7. Which of these is mentioned in the passage?
   A. the Kobe earthquake
   B. the expense of the project
   C. a major typhoon
   D. all of the above

8. What facilities does the airport have?
   A. 5 hotels
   B. 26 gift shops
   C. 35 restaurants
   D. 200 kids' rooms

INFERENCE

9. What will the passenger do next?
   A. read the report
   B. get something to eat
   C. board the plane
   D. go shopping for gifts

10. What did the reporter promise to do for the passenger?
    A. send him a copy of her article
    B. call him with news
    C. write him a letter
    D. meet him for lunch

Read this e-mail response to the reporter's newspaper article. Notice the bold words. Then match the bold words to their definitions below.

I found your report on the Kansai airport interesting. I wanted, however, to read more about the construction of the airport. You interviewed a passenger who was an architect. What a great **opportunity** to ask more questions about architecture! Instead, you interviewed him mainly about the airport's facilities.

Don't get me wrong. I think the facilities are **impressive**. The whole **atmosphere** is welcoming. But, let's not forget that this is an airport, not a hotel. Yes, the airport has **plenty** of restaurants and coffee shops. I travel a lot, and food is important. But I want to spend as little time in airports as possible.

The Kansai airport is a **spectacular** work of modern engineering. Did you know, for example, that the Kobe earthquake happened only 4 months after construction finished? This was a real test for the Kansai airport. There was no major **damage**. Now, that's impressive!

I have a suggestion about your next report. Why don't you write about famous **landmarks** in Japan? Or something **equally** interesting? People like to go **sightseeing**. I don't think people want to **explore** airports.

A.

1. atmosphere ___   **a.** travel around a place to learn about it
2. damage ___   **b.** to the same degree
3. equally ___   **c.** causing a feeling of respect
4. explore ___   **d.** harm from something bad
5. impressive ___   **e.** the way a place makes you feel

B.

1. landmarks ___   **a.** a chance to do something you would like to do
2. opportunity ___   **b.** a lot
3. plenty ___   **c.** very impressive or interesting
4. sightseeing ___   **d.** objects or buildings that can be seen easily, often important places
5. spectacular ___   **e.** visiting places as a tourist

DISCUSS THE THEME

Read these questions and discuss them with a partner. Share your ideas with the class.

1. What is the best airport you have seen? Give reasons.

2. Which do you prefer, more comfortable airplanes or better airports? Why?

CHAPTER 3

THE HISTORY OF AIRPORTS

◀ Plum Island Airfield in Newbury, Massachusetts
The oldest operating airfield in the USA

PREPARE TO LISTEN

Look at the picture above. Discuss these questions.

1. Describe the picture.

2. What do you think an airport must include?

WORD FOCUS 1

Match the words with their definitions.

accommodate	concrete	handling	muddy
aviation	expansion	ideal	

1. a hard substance that is used in building _____

2. filled or covered with soft, wet earth _____

3. dealing with something _____

4. the flying or building of aircraft _____

5. the act of becoming larger; growth _____

6. have enough space for something _____

7. perfect; the best possible _____

MAKE A PREDICTION

The first airports had runways made of concrete.

a. True   **b.** False

🎧 **Now listen to a museum tour guide. Check your prediction.**

CHECK YOUR COMPREHENSION

 Listen to the audio again and answer the questions. Circle your answers.

MAIN IDEA

1. What is the main topic?
   A. Airport design has changed through time.
   B. Airport traffic has decreased.
   C. Airport traffic has increased.
   D. Airports are complex and hi-tech.

DETAIL

2. According to the passage, what is a runway?
   A. the place where airplanes land
   B. the place where airplanes take off
   C. the most important structure at an airport
   D. all of the above

3. Concrete and grass are both ideal choices for a runway.
   A. True
   B. False

4. What is true about the first international airport?
   A. It was built in Italy.
   B. It opened in 1960.
   C. It was built in England.
   D. none of the above

5. Some airports started handling commercial traffic after World War I.
   A. True
   B. False

6. What happened around 1960?
   A. A world war in Europe ended.
   B. The first concrete runway was built.
   C. There were major changes in airport design.
   D. The first international airport opened.

7. Which of the following is **not** mentioned?
   A. Concrete runways can handle a lot of traffic.
   B. Concrete runways are good in all weather.
   C. Concrete runways are smooth.
   D. Concrete runways are inexpensive to build.

8. Which of these helped accommodate increased traffic?
   A. expansion of facilities
   B. more passenger buildings
   C. more runways
   D. all of the above

INFERENCE

9. Why does the tour guide mention Hong Kong International Airport?
   A. It was the first high-tech airport.
   B. It's an example of a big, beautiful airport.
   C. It was built on an artificial island.
   D. It's where they are for their museum tour.

10. What does the tour guide think about airport designers?
    A. They can't find good jobs.
    B. They should learn to fly planes.
    C. They have great jobs.
    D. They should design bigger airplanes.

WORD FOCUS 2

Read this visitor's e-mail response to the tour guide's presentation. Notice the bold words. Then match the bold words to their definitions below.

I visited the Aviation Museum with a group of student architects the other day. You gave us a tour of the museum. The information you presented was very interesting and **educational**. My favorite part was when you talked about airport design. I am studying to be an architect. I am interested in airports because my father is a **commercial** pilot. I think his job is exciting but very dangerous.

Often, he has to land planes during snowstorms. The **surface** of the **runway** can be a problem. There have been **improvements** in the way runways are designed and **laid**. This makes me feel better. We all want airplanes to land safely.

Once, I **considered** becoming a pilot. But, I chose architecture instead. I plan to use my **imagination** and knowledge to design better airports. **Currently**, we are learning about designing **terminals**. That is what I hope to work on in the future. I want to design terminals that can accommodate a lot of passengers.

I want to thank you for your interesting presentation. I hope to see you on my next visit to the museum.

A.
1. commercial ___
2. considered ___
3. currently ___
4. educational ___
5. imagination ___

   a. connected to learning; useful
   b. the ability to be creative
   c. at the present time; now
   d. connected with business
   e. thought about

B.
1. improvements ___
2. laid ___
3. runway ___
4. surface ___
5. terminals ___

   a. changes that make something better
   b. buildings where passengers begin or end their trips
   c. a strip of ground where aircraft take off and land
   d. put down; set in position
   e. the outside part or layer of something

DISCUSS THE THEME

Read these questions and discuss them with a partner. Share your ideas with the class.

1. What jobs related to airports or aviation would be most interesting?

2. What do you think airports of the future will look like?

VOCABULARY REVIEW

Fill in the blanks with words from each box.

atmosphere	improvements	landmark	opportunities

1. Kansai Airport is on an island. The airport is a world-famous _____.
2. I have had several _____ to travel through the Kansai Airport.
3. Some airports don't have a very good _____. They feel dark and crowded.
4. There have been many _____ in airports since 1960.

commercial	concepts	impressive	terminal

5. _____ aviation began after World War I. Before that time, airports were for military use.
6. Was there any damage to the _____ during the earthquake?
7. The architect used several new design _____ to prevent damage.
8. The design of the new airport was quite _____. It has wonderful facilities for passengers.

WRONG WORD

One word in each group does not fit. Circle the word.

1. runway	pilot	aviation	expansion
2. impressive	spectacular	educational	dramatic
3. presentation	design	construction	architect
4. board	muddy	take off	land
5. value	terminal	facilities	structure
6. slab	plenty	surface	concrete

Fill in the blanks with words from each box.

> imagination (*noun*)   imaginative (*adjective*)   imagine (*verb*)

1. That artist is very _____. He paints common objects in unusual ways.
2. I can't _____ the world without art. It would be a boring place to live.
3. Artists use their skill, creativity, and _____ to create great art.

> admiration (*noun*)   admirable (*adjective*)   admire (*verb*)

4. People _____ her work as an architect. She is one of the best designers in that office.
5. At a very young age, he showed an _____ ability to create beautiful art.
6. The young architects had great _____ for their professor.

WRAP IT UP

PROJECT WORK

Survey 2–4 people outside of class about airports they have used. Ask them the following questions:

- What airports have you used?
- What did you like about these airports? What did you not like?
- What would make airports better?

Present your findings to the class. If possible, find photos of the airports mentioned in the survey. Discuss the results with your classmates.

INTERNET RESEARCH

Go online and find information about a famous architect and the architect's projects. Find answers to the following questions:

- What is the architect's name? Date and place of birth? Type of training?
- What kinds of projects did he/she design? Where are they located? What is interesting about them?
- What do you think about this architect's work?

Print a photo of some of the architect's work, if possible. Present your information to the class.

MUSIC
WORLD MUSIC

The African Children's Choir

BEFORE YOU LISTEN

Answer these questions.

1. Why do you think the children in the picture are dressed this way?

2. Have you ever heard a choir? What kind of music did they sing?

3. What kinds of music do you like?

Chapter 1
Cesaria Evora: Barefoot Diva

◀ Cesaria Evora, 1941–

Prepare to Listen

Look at the picture above. Discuss these questions.

1. What is interesting about the woman in the picture?

2. Why do you think she dresses this way?

Word Focus 1

Match the words with their definitions.

composer	diva	on the air
distinguished	mourn	rhythmic

1. important and respected _____
2. feel great sadness, especially because of a death _____
3. having a regular and repeated sound _____
4. an important woman singer _____
5. broadcasting on the radio or television _____
6. a person who writes music _____

Make a Prediction

Cesaria Evora sings barefoot because she is very poor.

a. True   **b.** False

🎧 **Now listen to a radio program. Check your prediction.**

CHECK YOUR COMPREHENSION

 Listen to the audio again and answer the questions. Circle your answers.

MAIN IDEA

1. What is the main topic?
   - **A.** the life and music of the world's best singer
   - **B.** the life and music of a distinguished singer
   - **C.** Cesaria Evora's poor background
   - **D.** the music of Africa

DETAIL

2. What does the first listener want to know?
   - **A.** He wants to know about *morna* music.
   - **B.** He wants to know about the show.
   - **C.** He wants to know about Cesaria Evora.
   - **D.** He wants to know about African music.

3. Most Cape Verdeans are wealthy.
   - **A.** True
   - **B.** False

4. What is true about Cesaria Evora's early life?
   - **A.** Her father raised her.
   - **B.** She lived in New York.
   - **C.** She was born in the Canary Islands.
   - **D.** none of the above

5. Cesaria Evora's life experiences inspired her music.
   - **A.** True
   - **B.** False

6. What is **not** true about Cesaria Evora's family?
   - **A.** Her father played music.
   - **B.** Her uncle was a composer.
   - **C.** They are considered a musical family.
   - **D.** Her father became famous for his singing.

7. What is *morna*?
   - **A.** a modern type of music
   - **B.** English music
   - **C.** a traditional type of music
   - **D.** a happy type of music

8. What did Cesaria Evora earn because of her music?
   - **A.** fame
   - **B.** money
   - **C.** awards
   - **D.** all of the above

INFERENCE

9. What is true about Cesaria Evora?
   - **A.** She doesn't like to go back to Cape Verde.
   - **B.** She thinks about others' struggles.
   - **C.** She doesn't really sing barefoot.
   - **D.** She gave all her money to her brother.

10. What is true about the two listeners of the radio show?
    - **A.** They are big fans of music.
    - **B.** They are musicians.
    - **C.** They know a lot about Cesaria Evora.
    - **D.** They are from Cape Verde.

Read this e-mail about the radio program. Notice the bold words. Then match the bold words to their definitions below.

To: OXP Radio
Subject: your show about the Barefoot Diva

I'm usually at work when your show is on. I'm so glad that wasn't the **case** yesterday. I loved your show about Cesaria Evora. One thing surprised me: Cesaria sings barefoot to remind us that not everyone can **afford** shoes! What an amazing woman!

Maybe you've heard of another group of musicians that makes a difference—the African Children's Choir. This is a choir of young children, ages 7 to 12 years old. They all have **musical** gifts. All the children **earned** their places on the choir with their hard work.

Like Cesaria, their voices **match** their songs. When I hear these children sing, I forget about life's **disappointments**. Their music **inspires** people to want to sing. The choir gives concerts around the world. The money from the concerts goes to help Africa's 12 million orphans. Life is a **struggle** for the orphans. The choir uses the money it earns to help others. These wonderful children are Africa's future. They have worked hard for their **fame**.

I have a request. Can you do a show about the African Children's Choir? I think your listeners will really enjoy it. I will write you **shortly** with more information about this group.

Thank you and keep up the good work!

A.

1. afford ___   **a.** feelings of sadness because things did not go well
2. case ___   **b.** got something as a result of hard work
3. disappointments ___   **c.** the situation
4. earned ___   **d.** have enough money to be able to do something
5. fame ___   **e.** being known by many people

B.

1. inspires ___   **a.** causes a feeling of wanting to create something
2. match ___   **b.** soon
3. musical ___   **c.** a great effort
4. shortly ___   **d.** connected to music; good at music
5. struggle ___   **e.** are well suited to something else; fit

---

DISCUSS THE THEME

Read these questions and discuss them with a partner.

1. Who is your favorite singer? What type of music does that person sing?

2. In what ways can music inspire people?

CHAPTER 2
THE MUSIC OF GHANA

African musicians
in concert

PREPARE TO LISTEN

Look at the picture above. Discuss these questions.

1. Describe the people in the picture.
2. Have you ever heard African music? How would you describe it?

WORD FOCUS 1

Match the words with their definitions.

appeals to	equator	official	upbeat
audience	lyrics	tropical	

1. the imaginary line that divides the earth in half _____
2. is attractive or interesting to somebody _____
3. positive; happy _____
4. very hot and humid _____
5. the particular group of people who listen to, watch, or read something _____
6. the words of a song _____
7. accepted by the government or people in authority _____

MAKE A PREDICTION

The lecture discusses three types of popular music in Ghana.

a. True   **b.** False

🎧 **Now listen to part of a lecture on the music of Ghana. Check your prediction.**

Listen to the audio again and answer the questions. Circle your answers.

MAIN IDEA

1. What is the main topic?
    A. the climate and economy of Ghana
    B. Ghana's famous dance clubs
    C. two styles of music from Ghana
    D. Ghana's hip hop and rap artists

DETAIL

2. What two products from Ghana are mentioned?
    A. coffee and cacao
    B. gold and oil
    C. fish and bananas
    D. none of the above

3. How many languages are spoken in Ghana?
    A. 20
    B. 59
    C. 60
    D. 79

4. What characterizes highlife music?
    A. the use of drums and guitars
    B. its upbeat sound
    C. its rhythmic sound
    D. all of the above

5. What is hiplife?
    A. a popular performer in Ghana
    B. a combination of traditional and modern music
    C. a blend of modern hip hop and rap styles
    D. a young audience in Ghana

6. Highlife is a more traditional style of music.
    A. True
    B. False

7. Which languages are mentioned with hiplife?
    A. Twi, Hausa, Ga, and French
    B. German, English, and French
    C. English, Hausa, Twi, and Ga
    D. English, Hausa, and Chinese

8. What do some people criticize about hiplife songs?
    A. the drums
    B. the dances
    C. the lyrics
    D. the guitars

INFERENCE

9. What do some people believe about hiplife music?
    A. that it makes people behave better
    B. that it is causes artists to argue
    C. that it influences the way kids act
    D. that the audience is too young

10. What is the next lecture going to be about?
    A. the products of Nigeria
    B. a type of drum language
    C. the people of the Caribbean
    D. travel in West Africa

Read this student's e-mail about the lecture. Notice the bold words. Then match the bold words to their definitions below.

I wanted to write about the problem mentioned with hiplife and rap. First of all, I'm from Ghana. I love all kinds of music. However, I don't like anything that affects behavior **negatively**.

Highlhm music is **characterized by** its rhythm. Sadly, songs with bad lyrics are **increasingly** popular. Hiplife is a **relatively** new music style. I think it is a great addition to African music. But I also think artists should be careful with their language. Some of the songs are full of bad language. Some kids think it's OK to talk this way. Many people **blame** the music for the kids' **behavior**. We hear **arguments** against hiplife and rap music.

There are plenty of problems to fix in Africa. We should try to improve our **economy**. I don't think music should create more **battles**. Music should help people feel better. It should help us **communicate** our ideas and feelings but without the use of bad language!

A.
1. arguments ___
2. battles ___
3. behavior ___
4. blame ___
5. characterized by ___

a. the way that you act
b. described by typical qualities
c. the reasons that you give to support your opinions
d. fights; disagreements
e. believe that someone is the cause of something bad

B.
1. communicate ___
2. economy ___
3. increasingly ___
4. negatively ___
5. relatively ___

a. the operation of a country's money supply
b. in a bad way
c. make ideas known to other people
d. to a certain degree; more or less
e. more and more

DISCUSS THE THEME

Read these questions and discuss them with a partner. Share your ideas with the class.

1. Do you think too many songs have bad lyrics? Why or why not?

2. Why do you think musicians use bad lyrics?

CHAPTER 3
A WORLD MUSIC CONCERT

◀ Musician playing the kora

PREPARE TO LISTEN

Look at the picture above. Discuss these questions.

1. Do you play any musical instruments? Which ones?
2. What is the most unusual instrument you have seen? Describe it.

WORD FOCUS 1

Match the words with their definitions.

concert	strings	typical
ethnic	tune	version

1. a song or part of a song _____
2. connected with a group from a particular country _____
3. usual; having the qualities of a particular type _____
4. a new or different form of something _____
5. a performance of music _____
6. the pieces of thin wire on a musical instrument _____

MAKE A PREDICTION

The kora is a traditional instrument from Mali.

a. True   **b.** False

🎧 **Now listen to a conversation at a concert. Check your prediction.**

Listen to the audio again and answer the questions. Circle your answers.

MAIN IDEA

1. What is the main topic?
   A. Two friends discuss fusion in world music.
   B. Two friends discuss African music.
   C. Two friends discuss world instruments.
   D. Two friends discuss Cesaria Evora.

DETAIL

2. The term *world music* is used to describe only African music.
   A. True
   B. False

3. What is **not** considered ethnic music?
   A. folk music
   B. African music
   C. the typical Western music
   D. Latin music

4. What is true about the kora?
   A. It is a drum.
   B. It is a style of music.
   C. It has strings.
   D. It is 21 inches (53 centimeters) long.

5. The concert will include jazz music.
   A. True
   B. False

6. Which example of fusion in world music is mentioned?
   A. a jazz song from Cape Verde
   B. a love song from Mali
   C. a traditional song from the mountains of Peru
   D. an Indian folk tune used in a rap song

7. Which of these words means the same as *fuse*?
   A. join
   B. find
   C. tune
   D. fill

8. Which of the following is **not** true?
   A. Fusion combines elements from different styles.
   B. Some musicians continue to play traditional music.
   C. As the world changes, music changes.
   D. Fusion music is from only one culture.

INFERENCE

9. Why is it easier for musicians to fuse music today?
   A. Musicians can perform in concerts.
   B. Musicians have better instruments.
   C. Musicians have recorded music.
   D. Musicians are more creative.

10. The speakers don't like traditional music.
    A. True
    B. False

Read these online comments about the concert. Notice the bold words. Then match the bold words to their definitions below.

> A friend **recently** gave me a ticket to a world music concert as a birthday gift. I love music, but I didn't know much about world music. **Initially**, I didn't know what to expect. When the **show** started, I immediately liked the music. It **featured** many **elements** of traditional latin rhythm, but it also sounded very modern.
>
> The **musicians** were very good. They combined traditional and modern instruments, like the kora and the electric guitar. What a great combination! I think that no rules **apply** to good music. Musicians have **access** to music and instruments from around the world. They can mix anything they want. That's what these musicians did. They mixed **familiar** sounds with new sounds.
>
> Since the concert, my **taste** in music has changed. Now, I often listen to world music. I've become a big fan.

A.

1. access ___   **a.** the parts of something
2. apply ___   **b.** well-known
3. elements ___   **c.** relate to something
4. familiar ___   **d.** included something as an important part
5. featured ___   **e.** the ability to use something

B.

1. initially ___   **a.** what you like
2. musicians ___   **b.** a performance in front of an audience
3. recently ___   **c.** a short time ago
4. show ___   **d.** at the beginning; at first
5. taste ___   **e.** people who are good at writing or playing music

DISCUSS THE THEME

Read these questions and discuss them with a partner. Share your ideas with the class.

1. Have you ever gone to a concert? If yes, describe the experience.

2. What performers would you like to see in a concert?

VOCABULARY REVIEW

Fill in the blanks with words from each box.

apply	blame	disappointment	taste

1. The two brothers _____ each other for missing the concert. They didn't leave the house early enough.

2. Missing the concert was a big _____. Next time they will leave earlier.

3. My sister and I have different _____ in music. She likes classical music. I like jazz.

4. The old rules don't _____ to music today. Musicians combine many instruments.

arguments	elements	relatively	shortly

5. We arrived at the concert _____ before it started.

6. Some composers combine both new and old _____ in their music.

7. We hear all the same _____ about the way lyrics affect young people.

8. Instruments from different cultures are becoming _____ common.

WRONG WORD

One word in each group does not fit. Circle the word.

1. composer   musician   struggle   concert
2. official   rhythmic   upbeat   musical
3. diva   typical   distinguished   special
4. instrument   lyrics   battle   tune
5. equator   tropical   climate   mourn
6. audience   listeners   behavior   viewers

WORD FAMILIES

Fill in the blanks with words from each box.

increase (*noun*)	increasing (*adjective*)	increasingly (*adverb*)

1. Recently, there has been a big _____ in the price of concert tickets.
2. Toward the end, the music became _____ loud. It hurt our ears.
3. The _____ noise caused several people to leave early.

inspiration (*noun*)	inspirational (*adjective*)	inspire (*verb*)

4. Her good friends helped to _____ her in her singing career.
5. The story was _____. It described the positive changes in the singer's life.
6. Many composers find _____ in daily life experiences.

WRAP IT UP

PROJECT WORK

Choose a world music song you like. You may choose any type of song with lyrics. Answer the following questions:

- Who is the singer? Where is the singer from?
- What is the song about?
- Which instruments are used?

Describe the song to your classmates. If possible, write down the lyrics and bring a recording of the song to play for the class.

INTERNET RESEARCH

Go online and find information about the African Children's Choir or another ethnic music group. Find answers to the following questions:

- What type of music group is it? (choir, band, etc.)
- What kind of music do they sing or play?
- What is their background? (country of origin, brief history, etc.)
- What is most interesting about this group?

Print a picture of the group and bring a recording, if you can. Present your information to the class.

UNIT 5

HISTORY
EXPLORATION OF THE SEA

▲
Exploring underwater

BEFORE YOU LISTEN

Answer these questions.

1. What do you see in the picture? What is this man doing?

2. Have you ever been underwater in the ocean? Near what place was this?

3. What kinds of things can you see underwater?

CHAPTER 1
JACQUES-YVES COUSTEAU: MARINE SCIENTIST

Jacques-Yves Cousteau,
1910–1997

Look at the picture above. Discuss these questions.

1. Jacques-Yves Cousteau was a marine scientist. What do you know about him?
2. What do marine scientists study? What difficulties do they face?

WORD FOCUS 1

Match the words with their definitions.

breathing	marine	scuba	sunken ships
dive	navy	sea mammals	

1. boats that have gone down to the bottom of the sea _____
2. swimming underwater using a bottle of air _____
3. go underwater, often to look for things _____
4. connected with the sea _____
5. taking in air and blowing it out again _____
6. a part of the military that fights at sea on boats _____
7. marine animals, such as whales and dolphins, that give birth to live animals

_____

MAKE A PREDICTION

Jacques-Yves Cousteau had a popular radio show.

a. True   **b.** False

🎧 **Now listen to two students talk about a biology project. Check
your prediction.**

CHECK YOUR COMPREHENSION

 Listen to the audio again and answer the questions. Circle your answers.

MAIN IDEA

1. What is the main topic?
   A. Jacques-Yves Cousteau was a famous inventor.
   B. Jacques-Yves Cousteau did underwater research.
   C. One student looked for information about Jacques-Yves Cousteau.
   D. The students decide to do their biology project on Jacques-Yves Cousteau.

DETAIL

2. The two speakers are
   A. biologists
   B. classmates
   C. researchers
   D. teachers

3. Jacques-Yves Cousteau was
   A. a filmmaker
   B. a marine scientist
   C. an inventor of underwater equipment
   D. all of the above

4. "The Undersea World of Jacques Cousteau" is
   A. a research study
   B. a television series
   C. the title of a book
   D. a magazine article

5. Which of the following is **not** mentioned?
   A. strange fish
   B. sea mammals
   C. sunken ships
   D. fishing methods

6. Which statement is true about Jacques-Yves Cousteau?
   A. He was born in France.
   B. He was 70 when he died.
   C. He joined the French Army in 1933.
   D. He had a submarine called the *Calypso*.

7. Which of the following was **not** invented by Jacques-Yves Cousteau?
   A. a diving bell
   B. scuba equipment
   C. an underwater camera
   D. a two-person submarine

8. Jacques-Yves Cousteau wrote a well-known song about his boat.
   A. True
   B. False

INFERENCE

9. What will probably happen next?
   A. The students will begin work on the project.
   B. The students will take scuba lessons.
   C. The students will change the topic for their project.
   D. The students will travel on the *Calypso*.

10. Which of the following is probably true?
    A. The *Calypso* is now a sunken ship.
    B. Most people found Cousteau boring to talk to.
    C. People became marine scientists because of Cousteau.
    D. Cousteau's inventions are not used today.

Read this e-mail that Sarah sent to Jenny. Notice the bold words. Then match the bold words to their definitions below.

Hi Jenny!

I've been doing some research for our **biology project**. I think Cousteau is a great **choice** for our project. He's a really interesting man! Here's some information about his life from the Internet.

As we already know, Jacques-Yves Cousteau was born in France in 1910. He was always interested in the sea and machines, so he joined the navy in 1933. Later, he started exploring in his own boat, the *Calypso*. He became a famous **scientist**. He was known for his underwater research. He had a TV **series** in the 1970s. For the first time, people could see all kinds of **fascinating** fish, marine plants, and sea mammals up close.

At that time, there was not much marine **equipment** to use. So he **invented** what he needed to explore the underwater world—scuba equipment for long dives, an underwater camera, and a small **submarine**. He also found time to make movies and write books. He even won a few Oscars for his movies. John Denver, a popular singer in the 1970s, even wrote a song about his boat. It was a big **hit**. Cousteau died in 1997 at the age of 87. But people still remember him as a great underwater explorer and inventor.

These are some important facts about his life. Let's share our information in more detail on Thursday. See you then.

Sarah

A.
1. biology ___
2. choice ___
3. equipment ___
4. fascinating ___
5. hit ___

a. a song that is very popular
b. something needed for special activities
c. very interesting
d. something that has been chosen
e. the scientific study of living things

B.
1. invented ___
2. project ___
3. scientist ___
4. series ___
5. submarine ___

a. a type of boat that can go underwater
b. made something for the first time
c. TV programs showing at the same time each week
d. a person who studies science
e. a group activity to collect information for a class

DISCUSS THE THEME

Read these questions and discuss them with a partner.

1. What do you find most interesting about the sea?

2. What part of the sea would you like to explore?

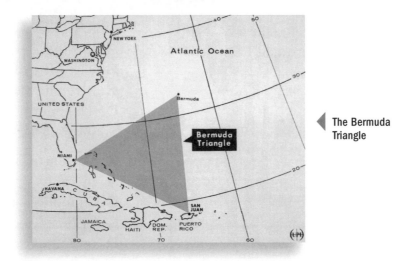

The Bermuda Triangle

PREPARE TO LISTEN

Look at the map above. Discuss these questions.

1. Describe the map. What is the name of this place?

2. This place is also called the "Devil's Triangle." Why do you think it has this name?

WORD FOCUS 1

Match the words with their definitions.

Caribbean	incidents	trace
devil	sail	

1. strange events _____
2. the most powerful bad spirit _____
3. a small sign that something happened _____
4. part of the ocean south of the U.S. with many islands _____
5. travel on water in a boat of any type _____

MAKE A PREDICTION

Airplanes have disappeared in the Bermuda Triangle.

a. True   **b.** False

🎧 **Now listen to a radio show about the Bermuda Triangle. Check your prediction.**

🎧 **Listen to the audio again and answer the questions. Circle your answers.**

MAIN IDEA

1. What is the main topic?
   A. David Martin wants to take a boat trip.
   B. One point of the Bermuda Triangle is Miami, Florida.
   C. Several planes disappeared in the Bermuda Triangle.
   D. Boats and planes disappear in the Bermuda Triangle.

DETAIL

2. What does David Martin host?
   A. a TV show
   B. a TV series
   C. a radio show
   D. a boat show

3. A lot of people in Florida have boats because
   A. they like to go fishing
   B. they enjoy taking boat trips
   C. the state is almost surrounded by water
   D. all of the above

4. The three points of the Bermuda Triangle are
   A. Puerto Rico, Miami, Aruba
   B. Puerto Rico, Miami, Bermuda
   C. Puerto Rico, Aruba, the Virgin Islands
   D. Puerto Rico, Miami, the Virgin Islands

5. The *Spray*
   A. disappeared in 1909
   B. was a U.S. Navy ship
   C. had 306 men on board
   D. disappeared in good weather

6. The *Star Tiger* and the *Star Ariel* were
   A. boats
   B. planes
   C. islands
   D. submarines

7. What is **not** true about the disappearance of U.S. Navy Flight 19?
   A. Weather conditions were bad.
   B. The plane disappeared without a trace.
   C. A rescue plane also disappeared.
   D. The pilot reported strange things happening.

8. David Martin says he will travel
   A. by car
   B. on foot
   C. by boat
   D. by plane

INFERENCE

9. Which statement about the Bermuda Triangle is probably true?
   A. Everyone disappears in the Bermuda Triangle.
   B. Nobody sails in the Bermuda Triangle.
   C. David Martin sailed in the Bermuda Triangle.
   D. There may be explanations for the disappearances.

10. Why does David Martin mention Joshua Slocum?
    A. David Martin knew Joshua Slocum.
    B. Joshua Slocum was David Martin's great-grandfather
    C. It is an example of a famous sailor's disappearance.
    D. It warns people never to fly an airplane alone.

Read this journal entry written by a man sailing alone from Miami to Bermuda. Notice the bold words. Then match the bold words to their definitions below.

May 24

Today has been a sunny day with a good wind. Weather **conditions** have been good. Tomorrow the weather is going to change. A storm is coming this way. I've been thinking about all the **strange** incidents in the Bermuda **Triangle**. I'm in the middle of the Bermuda Triangle now, so I'm trying not to feel nervous. I'm an **adventurous** person. I believe there is always an **explanation** for strange events. There are probably **clues** about missing boats. People just need to look harder. A **sailor** once told me about a strange event that happened to him. He was sailing at night toward a group of small **islands**. Suddenly, a group of whales **surrounded** his boat. The boat almost sank. Then, just as suddenly, the huge animals all **disappeared**. He felt really lucky that he and his boat had not disappeared without a trace. I think I have an explanation for this incident. I think the whales were probably just trying to be friendly. But I might have a different opinion if something like that happened to me!

A.

1. adventurous ___   **a.** the state of the environment
2. clues ___   **b.** went away with no trace
3. conditions ___   **c.** liking to try new and exciting things
4. disappeared ___   **d.** a reason for something
5. explanation ___   **e.** pieces of information that help to solve a problem

B.

1. islands ___   **a.** unusual or unexpected
2. sailor ___   **b.** pieces of land with water on all sides
3. strange ___   **c.** a person sailing a boat
4. surrounded ___   **d.** a shape with three straight sides and three angles
5. triangle ___   **e.** being all around something

DISCUSS THE THEME

Read these questions and discuss them with a partner.

1. Do you think there is something strange about the Bermuda Triangle? Would you feel nervous about flying or sailing in this area? Why or why not?

2. Strange incidents have happened in many parts of the world. What other examples have you heard about?

CHAPTER 3
THE HISTORY OF THE SUBMARINE

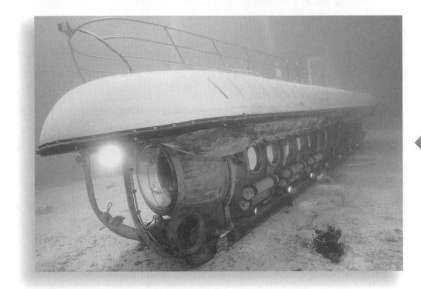

◄ A research submarine

PREPARE TO LISTEN

Look at the picture above. Discuss these questions.

1. What are submarines used for?

2. Would you like to be inside a submarine? Why or why not?

WORD FOCUS 1

Match the words with their definitions.

attacked	military	spy
impact	North Pole	

1. the most northern point of the Earth _____
2. moved against someone violently and with the plan of causing harm _____
3. an effect; an influence _____
4. related to the army, navy, etc. _____
5. try to get secret information _____

MAKE A PREDICTION

Submarines were invented in the twentieth century.

a. True   **b.** False

🎧 **Now listen to a lecture about submarines. Check your prediction.**

CHECK YOUR COMPREHENSION

 Listen to the audio again and answer the questions. Circle your answers.

MAIN IDEA

1. What is the main topic?
   A. ways submarines are used for research purposes
   B. military uses of submarines
   C. important inventions in modern history
   D. the history and uses of submarines

DETAIL

2. What was the topic of the previous class lecture?
   A. the history of submarines
   B. different kinds of submarines
   C. an accident to one submarine
   D. great inventions in modern history

3. A submarine sandwich is
   A. short and wide
   B. long and wide
   C. long and narrow
   D. narrow and deep

4. The earliest submarine was probably used about
   A. 80 years ago
   B. 100 years ago
   C. 400 years ago
   D. 800 years ago

5. Submarines were useful for military purposes because
   A. they are difficult to see
   C. they can do research
   B. they are long and narrow
   D. they have little privacy

6. The Germans built 100 submarines for use in World War II.
   A. True
   B. False

7. Which statement is **not** true about submarines?
   A. They are all large and long.
   B. They have traveled under the North Pole.
   C. They have sailed around the world.
   D. They can stay underwater for months.

8. Sailors on submarines
   A. have a lot of privacy
   B. have plenty of space
   C. live an easy life
   D. none of the above

INFERENCE

9. What is probably true about the submarine, *Kursk*?
   A. It is probably the biggest submarine.
   B. It probably had an accident.
   C. It probably returned to Russia.
   D. It probably sailed around the world.

10. In the past, submarine sailors could call their families from the ship.
    A. True
    B. False

Read the lecture notes that one student wrote in class. Notice the bold words. Then match the bold words to their definitions below.

Important inventions in modern history → the submarine (different kinds, history, important facts)

I. Word meaning
    sub = under, marine = ocean
    sub/submarine = underwater boat + type of sandwich (long and **narrow**)

II. History
    first sub used in the Ukraine in 17th century
    What did the first and **modern** subs have **in common**? spying!!
    American Civil War → not **effective** → subs **sank**, sailors died
    World War I & II → new **technologies**, new **weapons** → big impact
    e.g. German Navy → 1,000 subs

III. Research **Purposes**
    can stay underwater for months, can go anywhere
    have crossed the North Pole, have sailed around the world

IV. Life on a Sub
    not easy, little **space/privacy**, same food/faces
    but communication with families through technology
    Homework → Internet search → Russian sub Kursk, Aug 2000. What happened?

A.

1. effective ___   **a.** shared with each other
2. in common ___   **b.** the state of being alone
3. modern ___   **c.** producing the wanted result
4. narrow ___   **d.** of the present times
5. privacy ___   **e.** small in width

B.

1. purposes ___   **a.** guns, knives, bombs, etc.
2. sank ___   **b.** reasons for doing something
3. space ___   **c.** scientific knowledge used for practical purposes
4. technologies ___   **d.** gone down to the bottom of the water
5. weapons ___   **e.** available area

DISCUSS THE THEME

Read these questions and discuss them with a partner. Share your ideas with the class.

1. Would you enjoy the life of a sailor on a research submarine? What would be the advantages and disadvantages?

2. What will submarines be able to do in the future? What will submarines look like?

VOCABULARY REVIEW

WORDS IN CONTEXT

Fill in the blanks with words from each box.

biology	disappeared	equipment	invented

1. Some planes and boats have _____ without a trace in the Bermuda Triangle.
2. In our _____ class, we are studying sea mammals.
3. The first submarine was _____ in the Ukraine in the 17th century.
4. We need some special _____ to go scuba diving.

islands	privacy	purposes	technologies

5. Sailors on submarines do not have much _____ because there is so little space.
6. Modern submarines are used for both military and research _____ .
7. Submarines can sail between _____ and under the ice.
8. New _____ have improved communication on submarines between the sailors and their families.

WRONG WORD

One word in each group does not fit. Circle the word.

1. army	navy	triangle	military
2. invent	disappear	create	produce
3. guns	knives	weapons	conditions
4. series	clues	explanations	reasons
5. equipment	technology	sailor	communication
6. modern	strange	recent	new

Fill in the blanks with words from each box.

| explorer (*noun*) | exploration (*noun*) | explore (*verb*) |

1. Jacques-Yves Cousteau was a well-known _____ of sunken ships.
2. Modern submarines are used to _____ the ocean world under the sea.
3. Many people are interested in the _____ of the North and South Poles.

| fascination (*noun*) | fascinating (*adjective*) | fascinate (*verb*) |

4. Cousteau's movies of the colorful ocean world still _____ television viewers today.
5. Many people have a _____ for sea mammals, such as whales and dolphins.
6. I saw a _____ movie last week about strange incidents in different parts of the world.

WRAP IT UP

PROJECT WORK

Survey two people outside of class about their knowledge of marine life. Ask them the following questions:

- Have you ever been to an aquarium? If so, where?
- What marine animals or fish do you find most interesting?
- Have you ever heard of Jacques-Yves Cousteau? What do you know about him?

Present your findings to the class. Discuss the results with your classmates.

INTERNET RESEARCH

Go online and find information about one of the following topics relating to accidents, strange disappearances, or strange marine animals.

- the *Kursk* or the *USS Greeneville* submarine accidents
- the disappearance of the *USS Cyclops* or the *Mary Celeste* ghost ship
- the Tasman Sea Monster *or* the Scottish Loch Ness Monster

Print a photo, if you can. Present your information to the class.

HISTORY
SPIES

Spies and spy gadgets

BEFORE YOU LISTEN

Answer these questions.

1. The people in the picture are *spies*. What do spies do?

2. What kind of person makes a good spy?

3. What do you know about famous spies in history?

CHAPTER 1
CELEBRITY SPIES

Josephine Baker,
1906–1975

Marlene Dietrich,
1901–1992

PREPARE TO LISTEN

Look at the pictures above. Discuss these questions.

1. Have you ever heard of the women in the pictures? What might their jobs be?
2. Why do you think their pictures are included here?

WORD FOCUS 1

Match the words with their definitions.

antiwar	enemy	sharks	travel documents
brave	propaganda	shot down	

1. papers necessary for travel, such as a passport _____
2. information that a government uses to influence people, often not true _____
3. the army or country that you are fighting against _____
4. against war _____
5. made an airplane crash by shooting it with a weapon _____
6. large fish with sharp teeth _____
7. ready to do things that are dangerous _____

MAKE A PREDICTION

Josephine Baker stayed in Germany during World War II.

a. True   **b.** False

🎧 **Now listen to a classroom discussion about spies. Check your prediction.**

🎧 **Listen to the audio again and answer the questions. Circle your answers.**

MAIN IDEA

1. What is the main topic?
   A. where spies were in World War II
   B. the most famous spy in World War II
   C. why women were spies in World War II
   D. famous women spies of World War II

DETAIL

2. A *celebrity* is
   A. a famous person
   B. a dancer
   C. a cook
   D. a spy

3. Which of the following is **not** true?
   A. Josephine Baker was a dancer.
   B. Josephine Baker was French.
   C. Josephine Baker was an actress.
   D. Josephine Baker lived in Paris.

4. Josephine Baker helped the Nazis.
   A. True
   B. False

5. Marlene Dietrich was born in Germany.
   A. True
   B. False

6. How did Marlene Dietrich help the Americans during World War II?
   A. She sang propaganda songs in German.
   B. She sang propaganda songs in English.
   C. She acted in propaganda movies.
   D. She acted in the movie "The Blue Angel."

7. What OSS problem is mentioned?
   A. Sharks attacked submarines underwater.
   B. Weapons were killing sharks.
   C. Sharks attacked the enemy.
   D. Sharks attacked pilots in the water.

8. Which of the following is **not** true?
   A. Both Marlene Dietrich and Julia Child worked for the OSS.
   B. Julia Child invented a chemical to repel sharks.
   C. Julia Child was a famous chef during World War II.
   D. Julia Child's invention is still used today.

INFERENCE

9. Why was Josephine Baker able to hide information in her music sheets?
   A. The Nazis did not check celebrities too carefully.
   B. She was really a spy for the Nazis in France.
   C. She helped the Nazis leave the country of France.
   D. There were only a few Nazis in France.

10. Why might the space program need the chemical that Julia Child invented?
   A. People who work in the space program are often spies.
   B. People who work in the space program sometimes work with sharks.
   C. People who work in the space program sometimes land in the water.
   D. People who work in the space program are often celebrity chefs.

Read this student's e-mail response to the ideas presented in class. Notice the bold words. Then match the bold words to their definitions below.

> I think celebrities can be very good spies. They make good spies *because* they're famous. Their fame gives them access to people. Their fame lets them go places that ordinary people can't go.
>
> Celebrities can use their skills as spies. For example, a singer or an actor can **broadcast** propaganda. This can **influence** the enemy. This is what Marlene Dietrich did in World War II. She **recorded** antiwar songs in German. Some Germans heard her recordings and changed their thinking.
>
> Other celebrity skills help with spying. For example, Julia Child understood chemistry. Child invented a **chemical**. It helped people who landed in water after a plane **crash**. It **repelled** sharks. It kept sharks away from the people in the water. As a result, people **survived** because the sharks didn't attack them.
>
> Also, celebrities are often not in as much **danger** from the enemy. This is because the enemy knows them. They can even carry **secret** messages when the enemy is near. The enemy soldiers recognize the celebrity, so they won't stop the celebrity and look for hidden messages.
>
> Many celebrities did work as spies. For example, the French government **honored** Josephine Baker. They awarded her for her spy work during the war.

A.

1. broadcast ___
2. chemical ___
3. crash ___
4. danger ___
5. honored ___

   a. a substance
   b. gave respect to
   c. the possibility that something bad may happen
   d. send out radio or television programs
   e. an accident, as when a plane falls from the sky

B.

1. influence ___
2. recorded ___
3. repelled ___
4. secret ___
5. survived ___

   a. continued to live
   b. affect behavior or thinking
   c. kept away
   d. made a permanent version of a song
   e. hidden; not known about

DISCUSS THE THEME

Read these questions and discuss them with a partner.

1. What qualities did these women need to be good spies?

2. Do all celebrities make good spies? Why or why not?

CHAPTER 2
THE INTERNATIONAL SPY MUSEUM

The International Spy Museum
in Washington, DC

PREPARE TO LISTEN

Look at the picture above. Discuss these questions.

1. What might you learn about at a spy museum?
2. What would you like to learn about spying?

WORD FOCUS 1

Match the words with their definitions.

bugs	code-breaking	disguises	fingerprint
codes	devices	espionage	gadgets

1. another word for "spying" _____
2. tools or pieces of equipment _____
3. very small hidden recording devices _____
4. clothes or items such as eyeglasses to change the way you look _____
5. systems of secret symbols _____
6. figuring out codes _____
7. the pattern on the tips of fingers _____
8. small tools or machines, informal _____

MAKE A PREDICTION

The International Spy Museum is also a school for spies.

a. True   **b.** False

🎧 **Now listen to a radio program about a spy museum. Check your prediction.**

CHECK YOUR COMPREHENSION

 Listen to the audio again and answer the questions. Circle your answers.

MAIN IDEA

1. What is the main topic?
   A. The International Spy Museum has a lot of gadgets.
   B. The International Spy Museum has art exhibits.
   C. The International Spy Museum is a school for spies.
   D. The International Spy Museum has exhibits about spying.

DETAIL

2. Which of the following is **not** true?
   A. The International Spy Museum is in Washington, DC.
   B. The International Spy Museum is the only public spy museum.
   C. The International Spy Museum has the largest collection of cameras.
   D. The International Spy Museum has the largest collection of spy devices.

3. How many spy gadgets does The International Spy Museum have?
   A. over 200
   B. over 300
   C. over 500
   D. over 2,000

4. Who helped to make spy disguises?
   A. Native Americans
   B. Queen Elizabeth I
   C. people in the movie business
   D. The International Spy Museum

5. According to the speaker, some birds were spies.
   A. True
   B. False

6. According to the speaker, what helped the development of the computer?
   A. codes written in invisible ink
   B. codes recorded with cameras
   C. code-breaking techniques
   D. codes carried by pigeons

7. Which of the following is **not** true?
   A. A queen was a spy during World War II.
   B. A baseball player was a spy during World War II.
   C. A movie director was a spy during World War II.
   D. A singer was a spy during World War II.

8. You can buy your own spy equipment at The International Spy Museum.
   A. True
   B. False

INFERENCE

9. The Germans could not figure out the Navaho code during World War II.
   A. True
   B. False

10. The history of espionage starts with World War II.
    A. True
    B. False

**Read this e-mail about the program on the spy museum. Notice the bold words.
Then match the bold words to their definitions below.**

TO: WNFQ Radio

Subject: Your Program on the Spy Museum

I heard your radio **tour** of the spy museum, and I want to thank you. I decided to visit the museum myself last weekend. I had a great time.

I was impressed. There's a lot to see. The **collection** of spy gadgets is amazing. There are regular **exhibits** and special exhibits. My favorite regular exhibit was "School for Spies." I learned that I'm pretty **observant**—I notice details well. I could be a pretty good spy!

There was also a special exhibit on disguises. I didn't know about the **connection** between the movie business and the spy business. It makes sense, though. You can see some of the disguises at the museum.

I especially liked the information about code-breaking **techniques**. I learned that some of those systems helped in the **development** of the computer. I thought I knew a lot about the growth of the computer. But that was new to me. So were the **efforts** of the Navaho to create a code using their language. Their code helped to win the war.

The Spy Museum is a fun way for the **public**—both kids and adults—to **discover** the secret world of espionage and to learn a lot about history at the same time.

Thanks again for a great report.

A.

1. collection ___   **a.** learn about
2. connection ___   **b.** things that are done with difficulty
3. development ___   **c.** the relationship between two things
4. discover ___   **d.** the act of making a new product
5. efforts ___   **e.** a group of objects of a particular type

B.

1. exhibits ___   **a.** people in general
2. observant ___   **b.** ways of doing things
3. public ___   **c.** groups of objects shown in a museum
4. techniques ___   **d.** a short visit around a place
5. tour ___   **e.** able to see details

DISCUSS THE THEME

**Read these questions and discuss them with a partner. Share your ideas with
the class.**

1. What would you want to see at a spy museum?

2. Are museums a good way to learn about history? What are some other good ways?

CHAPTER 3
THE SCIENCE OF 007

◀ Agent 007 wearing a jetpack

PREPARE TO LISTEN

Look at the picture above. Discuss these questions.

1. Have you seen any of the James Bond movies? Which ones?
2. Can a jetpack really work? Explain your answer.

WORD FOCUS 1

Match the words with their definitions.

agent	facial recognition	sophisticated
binoculars	medical diagnosis	vision

1. the ability to see; sight _____
2. having a lot of experience in the world, especially in social situations _____
3. the identification of a disease _____
4. a person who works for certain government agencies _____
5. a technology for identifying faces _____
6. a device with two tubes for seeing far away _____

MAKE A PREDICTION

All of the gadgets in 007 spy movies really work.

a. True   **b.** False

🎧 **Now listen to part of a lecture on spy gadgets. Check your prediction.**

Listen to the audio again and answer the questions. Circle your answers.

MAIN IDEA

1. What is the main topic?
   A. Some of Agent 007's gadgets are real and some are not real.
   B. All of the actors in the 007 spy movies are real spies.
   C. Fake fingerprints really exist.
   D. Agent 007 uses a variety of devices and technologies.

DETAIL

2. Who wrote the 007 spy novels?
   A. Ian Fleming
   B. Dr. Goldfinger
   C. Fatima Blush
   D. James Bond

3. What are X-rays really used for?
   A. diagnosing illnesses
   B. seeing hidden weapons
   C. finding defects in metal
   D. all of the above

4. Fake fingerprints really exist.
   A. True
   B. False

5. Which of the following is true about the jetpack?
   A. It is not a real technology.
   B. It is now common transportation.
   C. It has no practical uses.
   D. It can lift a person 6,000 feet (1,800 meters).

6. What does Agent 007 use underwater to save his life?
   A. a jetpack
   B. a small breathing device
   C. night binoculars
   D. X-ray glasses

7. Which of the following does facial recognition do?
   A. It compares faces of pretty special people.
   B. It looks inside a person's face.
   C. It compares faces to a database.
   D. It uses images of people 20 years in the future.

8. Which of the following is **not** true?
   A. Facial recognition is a real technology.
   B. Night vision is a real technology.
   C. Night vision technology collects very small amounts of light.
   D. Facial recognition technology lets you see in the dark.

INFERENCE

9. You need expensive materials to make fake fingerprints.
   A. True
   B. False

10. How do fake fingerprints work?
    A. They hide a person's face.
    B. They make your fingers disappear.
    C. They make a person's hands warmer.
    D. They use another person's fingerprints.

Read this student's summary of the lecture. Notice the bold words. Then match the bold words to their definitions below.

> Today, we learned about spy gadgets in the James Bond movie series. A lot of the movies were made a long time ago. It's surprising how advanced some of the gadgets are. Some really work. Some don't. But most of them are pretty incredible. There's quite a **variety** of devices, from X-ray glasses to night vision. Of course, Bond is a very sophisticated guy. His gadgets have to be pretty advanced, too.
>
> One device that really works are the **fake** fingerprints. Bond wears fake fingerprints made from **ordinary** rubber. Fake fingerprints really exist. They can **fool** real **scanners**. Facial recognition technology really works, too. A device scans a person's face and records features. These features include the size of the nose or the distance between the eyes. Then it compares the features to a computer **database**. The database contains information on millions of faces. X-ray glasses aren't real, but X-rays have a lot of **practical** uses. They're used in **industry** to find **defects** in metal.
>
> Bond's enemies use incredible gadgets, too. One uses night binoculars. This is a real technology. Night vision **amplifies** light in the dark. It increases tiny amounts of light so you can see.

A.

1. amplifies ___   **a.** make somebody believe something that is not true
2. database ___   **b.** a large collection of information on a computer
3. defects ___   **c.** things that are wrong
4. fake ___   **d.** increases; makes bigger
5. fool ___   **e.** not real

B.

1. industry ___   **a.** useful
2. ordinary ___   **b.** different types of things
3. practical ___   **c.** common; not special or unusual
4. scanners ___   **d.** machines used to examine things
5. variety ___   **e.** the production of things

DISCUSS THE THEME

Read these questions and discuss them with a partner. Share your ideas with the class.

1. What is your favorite gadget in the James Bond movies?

2. Think of a new spy gadget. What does it do? How does it work?

VOCABULARY REVIEW

WORDS IN CONTEXT

Fill in the blanks with words from each box.

broadcast	danger	development	discover

1. You can _____ new things at a museum. For example, you can learn about the history of spying.

2. The Americans _____ Marlene Dietrich's songs to Germany.

3. Josephine Baker was in _____ during World War II because she was a spy.

4. Code-breaking during World War II helped the _____ of computer technology.

amplify	database	efforts	fool

5. The French honored Josephine Baker for her spy work. Her _____ helped save lives.

6. Facial recognition technology uses a/an _____ with facial features such as nose size.

7. Some spies use disguises to _____ the enemy.

8. Night vision technology can _____ light so that there is more of it.

WRONG WORD

One word in each group does not fit. Circle the word.

1. sharks   pigeons   dogs   codes
2. gadget   enemy   device   tool
3. observant   careful   fake   smart
4. public   ordinary   common   practical
5. collection   exhibit   group   chemical
6. binoculars   cameras   scanners   techniques

Fill in the blanks with words from each box.

| influence (*noun*) | influential (*adjective*) | influence (*verb*) |

1. During World War II, Marlene Dietrich tried to _____ the enemy with her music.
2. Sometimes music can have a positive _____ on people.
3. Dietrich's music helped to end the war. She was a very _____ person.

| observation (*noun*) | observant (*adjective*) | observe (*verb*) |

4. A good spy needs to be very _____.
5. Spies _____ people carefully. They can give good descriptions later on.
6. The woman made a careful _____ of the situation. Then she wrote a detailed report.

WRAP IT UP

PROJECT WORK

Survey two people outside of class about spies. Ask them the following questions:

- Who makes better spies, men or women? Why?
- Do celebrities make good spies? Why or why not?
- What kind of person makes the best spy?

Present your findings to the class. Discuss the results with your classmates.

INTERNET RESEARCH

Go online and find information about a famous spy. It can be a modern spy or a spy in history. It can be a real spy or a spy in a movie or book. Find answers to the following questions:

- What is the spy's name? What country or organization did the spy work for?
- Why is this spy famous?
- Did this person use any gadgets? How did they work?

Print a photo of the spy or the spy's gadgets, if you can. Present your information to the class.

CULTURAL STUDIES
JAPAN

The Meiji Jingu entrance

BEFORE YOU LISTEN

Answer these questions.

1. Do you know anyone who has visited Japan? What do you know about Japan?

2. Do you know the names of any artists, musicians, or movies from Japan?

3. What would you like to visit in Japan?

CHAPTER 1
HOKUSAI: MASTER PRINTMAKER

The Great Wave
by Hokusai

PREPARE TO LISTEN

Look at the picture above. Discuss these questions.

1. Describe what you see in the picture.
2. This type of art is called a *print*. Do you know how prints are made?

WORD FOCUS 1

Match the words with their definitions.

accessible	master	sketchbooks
carved	series	*ukiyo-e*

1. cut a shape into a block of wood _____
2. practice books for drawing _____
3. a style of Japanese painting _____
4. a set of something, such as pictures _____
5. available; easy to get _____
6. a person who has great skill at doing something _____

MAKE A PREDICTION

The artist Hokusai made many prints about Mt. Fuji.

a. True   **b.** False

🎧 **Now listen to a class discussion about the Japanese artist Hokusai. Check your prediction.**

Listen to the audio again and answer the questions. Circle your answers.

MAIN IDEA

1. What is the main topic?
   - **A.** Hokusai lived to be almost 90 years old.
   - **B.** Hokusai used special tools to carve wood.
   - **C.** Hokusai is famous for his prints about everyday life.
   - **D.** Most people could not afford to buy Hokusai's prints.

DETAIL

2. When was Hokusai born?
   - **A.** 1670
   - **B.** 1760
   - **C.** 1849
   - **D.** 1894

3. To make a print, Hokusai first carved a drawing in
   - **A.** stone
   - **B.** wood
   - **C.** ice
   - **D.** paper

4. Why did printmaking make art more accessible?
   - **A.** It was fast and inexpensive.
   - **B.** Many copies were made from one carving.
   - **C.** Copies were less expensive.
   - **D.** all of the above

5. Who was Shunsho?
   - **A.** Hokusai's teacher
   - **B.** Hokusai's student
   - **C.** Hokusai's father
   - **D.** Hokusai's favorite actor

6. According to the speaker, what does *floating world* refer to?
   - **A.** life on the ocean
   - **B.** types of boats
   - **C.** everyday life
   - **D.** ways to grow rice

7. Hokusai's most typical prints were made between 1830 and 1840.
   - **A.** True
   - **B.** False

8. Hokusai used his sketchbooks to practice.
   - **A.** True
   - **B.** False

INFERENCE

9. What was the main reason Hokusai made 13 sketchbooks?
   - **A.** He really liked to draw.
   - **B.** He liked drawing more than printmaking.
   - **C.** He wanted to teach young artists.
   - **D.** He needed to practice for his woodcarving.

10. Why did Hokusai make the series about Mt. Fuji?
    - **A.** to show that the way we see things changes
    - **B.** to show that nature never changes
    - **C.** to show that nature is a symbol of Japan
    - **D.** to show more examples of everyday life

Read this summary of the class discussion. Notice the bold words. Then match the bold words to their definitions below.

> Hokusai was a Japanese artist. He was born in 1760 and died in 1849. He lived in what is now Tokyo. He made prints and was a painter, too. He was very **talented**. He **produced** many works of art and was a master at making prints. Printmaking was a fast and inexpensive way to make copies. It took a lot of skill to make the **original** wood carving, though.
>
> In 1775, he went to study with an artist named Shunsho. Hokusai worked in a style called *ukiyo-e*. This means "pictures of the floating world." "Floating world" means "everyday life," for example, people cooking or growing rice. Hokusai made thousands of prints. He was very **prolific**. It's **estimated** he made around 30,000 prints.
>
> He also made drawings in 13 sketchbooks. He **demonstrated** many techniques. He wanted to teach young artists. He continued to **compile** the sketchbooks for 65 years.
>
> Hokusai did a series of prints called "The Thirty-Six Views of Mount Fuji." The 36 prints are all different. He made the prints to **express** how some things don't change. Our **perception** changes. He was interested in **portraying** the power of nature.

A.

1. compile ___	**a.** showed how to do something
2. demonstrated ___	**b.** the first one; not a copy
3. estimated ___	**c.** made a guess about the amount of something
4. express ___	**d.** collect and put together
5. original ___	**e.** let people know what you are thinking or feeling

B.

1. perception ___	**a.** showing something in a certain way
2. portraying ___	**b.** making a lot of something
3. produced ___	**c.** the way you see or understand something
4. prolific ___	**d.** very good at something not everyone can do
5. talented ___	**e.** made something using skill

DISCUSS THE THEME

Read these questions and discuss them with a partner.

1. Imagine Hokusai is alive today. What would he make prints of to show "everyday life"?

2. Think of a place in nature you know well. Describe how it looks in different seasons, at different times of day, and so on.

CHAPTER 2
JAPANESE GARDENS

◀ A Japanese garden

PREPARE TO LISTEN

Look at the picture above. Discuss these questions.

1. How would you describe the Japanese garden? What is in it?
2. Have you ever been to a Japanese garden? What was it like?

WORD FOCUS 1

Match the words with their definitions.

| garden | monks | stones |
| lantern | raked | tortoise |

1. an animal that has a hard shell and moves very slowly _____
2. moved with a garden tool _____
3. a type of lamp, often one that is carried _____
4. men who live in a religious group _____
5. a place with flowers and trees _____
6. small pieces of rock, often smooth and round _____

MAKE A PREDICTION

There is only one kind of Japanese garden.

a. True   **b.** False

🎧 **Now listen to part of an audio tour at a Japanese garden. Check your prediction.**

🎧 **Listen to the audio again and answer the questions. Circle your answers.**

MAIN IDEA

1. What is the main topic?
   A. Japanese gardens represent nature.
   B. Japanese gardens all look the same.
   C. Japanese gardens have beautiful plants.
   D. Japanese gardens are very simple.

DETAIL

2. Which of these words does **not** describe a Japanese garden?
   A. noisy
   B. quiet
   C. elegant
   D. calm

3. Everything in a Japanese garden
   A. is small
   B. is modern
   C. has a meaning
   D. is the same color

4. According to the speaker, what are the natural elements?
   A. the male lion and the female lion
   B. dark and light
   C. long life and good health
   D. earth, water, fire, and wind

5. The stone lions at the entrance protect the garden.
   A. True
   B. False

6. In a dry garden
   A. water flows around rocks
   B. water only goes under bridges
   C. rocks or sand are used instead of water
   D. there isn't enough water for the plants

7. Why are stones and sand raked in a dry garden?
   A. to give jobs to the monks
   B. to make them look like flowers
   C. to dry the stones and sand after it rains
   D. to make them look like flowing water

8. All Japanese gardens must look the same way.
   A. True
   B. False

INFERENCE

9. According to the speaker, what is the best season to visit?
   A. summer when there are colorful flowers
   B. winter when there is snow on the pine trees
   C. spring and fall when the trees are colorful
   D. all of the above

10. According to the speaker, is it important where you stand?
    A. Yes, you should stand at the entrance.
    B. Yes, you should stand in the center.
    C. No, it looks the same everywhere.
    D. No, it is enjoyable from different places.

Read this student's journal entry about the tour. Notice the bold words. Then match the bold words to their definitions below.

I think it's interesting that Japanese gardens are **representations** of **nature**. They present natural elements in an artistic way. They are a quiet place for people to go to **reflect on** their lives or to **meditate**. There are some **essential** elements that **make up** a Japanese garden. All things in the garden are put there for a reason. Everything in the garden has a meaning. A lot of things represent life, like water and a type of fish called koi.

My favorite part was the dry garden. In a dry garden, there is no water. Small stones or sand take the place of water. The rocks or sand are **arranged** to look like flowing water. Monks developed this type of garden.

There are many styles of Japanese gardens. Some are simple. Some are complex. All are very **elegant**. All of the gardens use a **combination** of the same basic elements. Garden designers must follow certain rules to make sure the elements are there. But, they have some freedom. They can be creative.

The elements in a garden are arranged so that there is something beautiful to observe any day of the year. For example, in summer, there are colorful flowers. In winter, there is snow on the dark pine trees. I like the idea that the garden should be **pleasing** wherever you are.

A.
1. arranged ___   **a.** important and necessary
2. combination ___   **b.** put in a certain way
3. elegant ___   **c.** combine together to form something
4. essential ___   **d.** having style, good design
5. make up ___   **e.** a way of putting two or more things together

B.
1. meditate ___   **a.** making someone feel happy
2. nature ___   **b.** spend time thinking in a special calm way, often as part of religious training
3. pleasing ___   **c.** think carefully about something
4. reflect on ___   **d.** all the things in the world that were not made by people
5. representations ___ **e.** things used to show something else

DISCUSS THE THEME

Read these questions and discuss them with a partner. Share your ideas with the class.

1. What do you think is interesting about a Japanese garden?

2. Why do you think water is used to represent life?

CHAPTER 3
MANGA COMICS

A drawing from a manga comic ▶

 ◀ Reading manga comics

PREPARE TO LISTEN

Look at the pictures above. Discuss these questions.

1. Have you read any manga comics? What were they about?
2. How would you describe the characters?

WORD FOCUS 1

Match the words with their definitions.

action	fans	speech bubbles
comic books	reminds	sweat

1. the water that comes out of your skin _____
2. excitement and movement, especially fighting _____
3. magazines that use drawings to tell stories _____
4. circles with words inside to show what people are saying _____
5. people who like something very much _____
6. makes someone remember something _____

MAKE A PREDICTION

Manga comics were created in the 1950s.

a. True   **b.** False

🎧 **Now listen to a news story on the radio about manga comics. Check your prediction.**

Listen to the audio again and answer the questions. Circle your answers.

MAIN IDEA

1. What is the main topic?
   A. who reads manga comics
   B. what manga comics are like
   C. where fans read manga comics
   D. when manga comics became popular

DETAIL

2. When did manga comics begin?
   A. about 10 years ago
   B. about 30 years ago
   C. about 50 years ago
   D. about 100 years ago

3. Why do artists use different shapes for speech bubbles?
   A. It shows which character is talking.
   B. It shows what a character will do next.
   C. It shows new parts of the story.
   D. It shows how the character is feeling.

4. Speed lines show where characters are going.
   A. True
   B. False

5. Why do artists use a drawing again?
   A. It shows how a character is feeling.
   B. It shows what will happen next.
   C. It reminds the reader what happened earlier.
   D. It shows the action.

6. Artists use sweat drops to show a character is nervous.
   A. True
   B. False

7. A character has very big eyes. The character is probably
   A. angry
   B. confused
   C. female
   D. embarrassed

8. Why are some manga magazines called telephone books?
   A. They are boring.
   B. They are thick.
   C. They are exciting.
   D. They are popular.

INFERENCE

9. Why do all manga comics look similar?
   A. The artists are not very creative.
   B. Only one artist draws all the manga comics.
   C. All the characters are related.
   D. They all use the same symbols and style.

10. Which of the following is probably true?
    A. Manga fans don't like thick manga magazines.
    B. Manga fans buy the next magazine right away.
    C. Manga fans are often late for work.
    D. Manga fans are all young.

Read this student's e-mail about the news story. Notice the bold words. Then match the bold words to their definitions below.

To: WXSL radio
Re: Manga comics

Your story on manga comic books was terrific. I knew they were popular in Japan. I didn't know that manga style is a **mixture** of Japanese and foreign styles of drawing. I was surprised they were created in Japan in the 1950s. I thought they were more recent. All manga share certain **characteristics**. I never thought about the techniques the artists use. It's cool how artists use **distinct shapes** for speech bubbles and thought bubbles to show how a character is feeling. Some manga have thought bubbles that look like an **explosion**. We see that, and we know the character feels angry. I also like the way artists use small **speed** lines to show the direction the characters are moving. Or, how artists use a drawing again to show a character is remembering something. It's true that characters from manga comics look very **similar**. They all have small noses and **tiny** mouths. I never thought about how all manga artists use the same symbols. The sweat drops on the face show the character is **confused**. Little lines on the face show the character is **embarrassed**.

Manga are becoming popular around the world. Thanks for the story about manga.

A.
1. characteristics ___
2. confused ___
3. distinct ___
4. embarrassed ___
5. explosion ___

a. clearly different
b. nervous; anxious in front of other people
c. qualities that are typical of something
d. a sudden burst or loud noise
e. not able to understand something clearly

B.
1. mixture ___
2. shapes ___
3. similar ___
4. speed ___
5. tiny ___

a. the same in many ways
b. the outer forms of things, such as circles or squares
c. fast movement
d. very small
e. a combination of two or more things

DISCUSS THE THEME

Read these questions and discuss them with a partner. Share your ideas with the class.

1. Think of some other ways manga artists could show feelings in manga comics. What would you do?

2. Why do you think manga comics are so popular?

VOCABULARY REVIEW

WORDS IN CONTEXT

Fill in the blanks with words from each box.

arranged	demonstrated	reflect on	produced

1. In his sketchbooks Hokusai _____ how to draw people and animals.
2. The rocks were _____ to look like flowing water.
3. Hokusai _____ around 30,000 prints altogether.
4. Some people like to go to Japanese gardens to sit and _____ their lives.

essential	mixture	perception	similar

5. The characters in manga comics are very _____. They are drawn in the same way.
6. Water is one of the _____ elements of a Japanese garden.
7. Hokusai thought that our _____ of a mountain is different from season to season.
8. Manga comics are a/an _____ of Japanese and foreign ways of drawing.

WRONG WORD

One word in each group does not fit. Circle the word.

1.	common	original	ordinary	usual
2.	style	compile	characteristics	technique
3.	lose	forget	leave	remind
4.	awful	terrible	pleasing	unpleasant
5.	limit	restrict	express	prevent
6.	careful	talented	alert	observant

WORD FAMILIES

Fill in the blanks with words from each box.

expression (*noun*)	expressive (*adjective*)	express (*verb*)

1. Hokusai wanted to _____ the idea that mountains and other things in nature don't change.

2. A Japanese garden is an _____ of Japanese ideas about nature.

3. The print was very _____. It showed the power of nature in a bad storm.

confusion (*noun*)	confusing (*adjective*)	confused (*adjective*)

4. Manga artists use special lines and symbols in the drawings. That way there is no _____ about what is happening.

5. In manga, a _____ character has sweat drops on the face.

6. The meaning of the manga symbols is clear to readers. The symbols aren't at all _____.

WRAP IT UP

PROJECT WORK

Work in a small group. Brainstorm a short story for a manga comic. Choose one part of the story to draw. Use the techniques manga artists use.

- Where does the story happen? Who are the characters?
- What happens in this part of the story?
- How are the characters feeling in each part?

Present your story to the class or to another group.

INTERNET RESEARCH

Go online and find information about a Japanese printmaker or garden. Find answers to the following questions:

- What is the name of the artist? *or* What is the name of the garden?
- When did this person live? *or* Where is the garden?
- Describe the artists work. *or* Describe the garden.

Print a photo, if you can. Present your information to the class or in groups.

TRANSPORTATION
HISTORY OF FLIGHT

An early bi-plane

A modern airliner

BEFORE YOU LISTEN

Answer these questions.

1. What do you know about the history of flight?

2. Who were the first people to fly? What did they fly in?

3. In what ways have airplanes changed over the years?

CHAPTER 1
ALBERTO SANTOS-DUMONT

Alberto Santos-Dumont,
1873–1932

PREPARE TO LISTEN

Look at the picture above. Discuss these questions.

1. Describe the picture. When do you think this photo was taken?
2. Why do you think Santos-Dumont was important in the history of flight?

WORD FOCUS 1

Match the words with their definitions.

aircraft	hot-air balloons	vehicles
airship	unassisted	Wright brothers

1. with no help _____
2. things which transport people from place to place _____
3. large balloons filled with air, which carry a basket of people _____
4. a plane or any vehicle that can fly _____
5. a large balloon aircraft that can be steered _____
6. two men who flew the first plane in 1903 _____

MAKE A PREDICTION

Alberto Santos-Dumont was famous in the early 1900s.

a. True   **b.** False

🎧 **Now listen to a discussion about Alberto Santos-Dumont. Check your prediction.**

Listen to the audio again and answer the questions. Circle your answers.

MAIN IDEA

1. What is the main topic?
   A. Alberto Santos-Dumont was an inventor.
   B. Alberto Santos-Dumont was an aviation pioneer.
   C. Alberto Santos-Dumont was in the Brazilian Air Ministry.
   D. Alberto Santos-Dumont was from a small town.

DETAIL

2. Alberto Santos-Dumont was born in
   A. France
   B. Germany
   C. Brazil
   D. the United States

3. How old was Santos-Dumont when he went to Paris?
   A. 18
   B. 19
   C. 21
   D. 23

4. Why is Santos-Dumont called the Father of Aviation in Brazil?
   A. He flew his first plane in Brazil.
   B. He started the Brazilian Air Ministry.
   C. He built and flew the first practical airship.
   D. He was the father of the Wright brothers.

5. In 1901, Santos-Dumont flew his airship around the Eiffel Tower in Paris.
   A. True
   B. False

6. Why was Santos-Dumont's flight in 1901 important?
   A. He remained in the air.
   B. He was able to steer and control the airship.
   C. It took him less than 30 minutes.
   D. all of the above

7. An airplane is an example of a heavier-than-air vehicle.
   A. True
   B. False

8. What happened on November 12, 1906, in Paris?
   A. Santos-Dumont flew his airship farther than before.
   B. Santos-Dumont flew with the Wright brothers.
   C. Santos-Dumont made the first public flight in an airplane.
   D. Santos-Dumont began selling heavier-than-air vehicles.

INFERENCE

9. Why was there a controversy?
   A. Santos-Dumont didn't really fly his airplane unassisted.
   B. The Wright brothers' flight was in a lighter-than-air aircraft.
   C. The Wright brothers' flight was later than Santos-Dumont's.
   D. The public didn't see the Wright brothers' 1903 flight.

10. What makes Santos-Dumont special as an aviation pioneer?
    A. People watched him fly his airplane around the Eiffel Tower.
    B. Santos-Dumont's airship was beautiful to see.
    C. He flew hot-air balloons, airships, and airplanes.
    D. Santos-Dumont liked to enter competitions.

Read this summary of the discussion about Santos-Dumont. Notice the bold words. Then match the bold words to their definitions below.

Alberto Santos-Dumont was born in Brazil. When he was 18, he went to Paris to study. Some people call him the Father of **Aviation** because he designed and flew the first practical airships. These were also called dirigibles. In 1901, he flew around the Eiffel Tower in Paris. He did it in less than 30 minutes. He was able to **remain** in the air and **steer** his airship. He showed the world that **routine**, controlled flight was possible. He was a **pioneer** in aviation. He became very famous.

At first, he worked on airships. Then he **shifted** his attention to the **challenge** of making an airplane. On November 12, 1906, in Paris, he made the first public flight with an airplane. He flew 715 feet (220 meters). He became internationally famous again.

There was a **controversy** because most people didn't know about the Wright brothers' 1903 flight. So, many people thought Santos-Dumont did it first. He **claimed** his was the first unassisted flight. Many people, especially in Brazil, still consider him the inventor of the airplane. He had many **accomplishments**. He died in Brazil in 1932. In 1955, the Brazilian government added his name to the Brazilian Air Ministry.

A.

1. accomplishments ___   **a.** something difficult to do
2. aviation ___   **b.** things you succeed in doing; achievements
3. challenge ___   **c.** public disagreement about something
4. claimed ___   **d.** said that something was true
5. controversy ___   **e.** the flying or building of aircraft

B.

1. pioneer ___   **a.** usual, normal
2. remain ___   **b.** control the direction a vehicle is going
3. routine ___   **c.** changed, directed in a new way
4. shifted ___   **d.** stay
5. steer ___   **e.** one of the first people to do something

DISCUSS THE THEME

Read these questions and discuss them with a partner.

1. Who do you think should be known for the "first flight"? Why?

2. Alberto Santos-Dumont was an aviation pioneer. What other pioneers do you know?

CHAPTER 2
KITTY HAWK, NORTH CAROLINA, U.S.A.

The Wright brothers and their airplane

PREPARE TO LISTEN

Look at the picture above. Discuss these questions.

1. What do you know about the Wright brothers?

2. The Wright brothers chose Kitty Hawk on the coast of North Carolina for their first flight. Why do you think they chose that place?

WORD FOCUS 1

Match the words with their definitions.

crash landing	sand dunes	weather station
gliders	sandy	

1. made up of small grains, like at the beach _____
2. a plane stopping on the ground in a dangerous way _____
3. light airplanes that fly on air and do not have engines _____
4. an office that collects weather information for an area _____
5. low hills of sand by the ocean or in the desert _____

MAKE A PREDICTION

The Wright brothers chose Kitty Hawk because it was a very windy place.

a. True   **b.** False

🎧 **Now listen to part of a lecture in a geography class. Check your prediction.**

Listen to the audio again and answer the questions. Circle your answers.

MAIN IDEA

1. What is the main topic?
   A. Kitty Hawk is famous because of the Wright brothers.
   B. Kitty Hawk used to be called Chickahawk.
   C. Kitty Hawk is a very old town in North Carolina.
   D. Kitty Hawk is a small town in the United States.

DETAIL

2. The Wright brothers' first flight lasted
   A. 2 seconds
   B. 12 seconds
   C. 22 seconds
   D. 120 seconds

3. The Wright brothers were from
   A. Washington, DC
   B. Ohio
   C. New York
   D. North Carolina

4. What was the Wright brothers' job?
   A. They owned a bicycle shop.
   B. They owned a bakery shop.
   C. They owned a small airport.
   D. They owned a weather station.

5. Why did they end up in North Carolina?
   A. It was warm there.
   B. It had beautiful parks.
   C. It was windy.
   D. It had big cities.

6. The U.S. Weather Bureau did not have the information they needed.
   A. True
   B. False

7. When is it windy in Kitty Hawk?
   A. July and September
   B. August and September
   C. September and October
   D. November and December

8. Which of the following is **not** mentioned about Kitty Hawk?
   A. telegraph
   B. mail every day
   C. good food
   D. friendly people

INFERENCE

9. Why did the Wright brothers want a small town?
   A. They didn't like people.
   B. They were hiding from the police.
   C. They wanted to start a new bicycle shop.
   D. They wanted to work in secret.

10. Which of the following describes the Wright brothers' flight?
    A. They reached their goal.
    B. They were never able to reach their goal.
    C. Their flight was not important.
    D. Thousands of people watched the flight.

Read this student's summary of the lecture. Notice the bold words. Then match the bold words to their definitions below.

Kitty Hawk is in North Carolina. It's famous for one reason. On December 17, 1903, the Wright brothers made their first airplane flight near Kitty Hawk. This was a big **moment** in the history of flight. Their flight **lasted** only 12 seconds. It didn't go very far, but it left the **ground** by its own power. The Wrights spent four years in North Carolina working toward their **goal**.

The Wright brothers were from Dayton, Ohio. They owned a bicycle shop, but they were interested in flying. No one had made much **progress** learning to fly. They decided to try. They built gliders, but they needed a place to fly them. They looked for a **location** with good winds for flying. This is how they **ended up** in North Carolina.

The Wright brothers **contacted** the U.S. Weather Bureau. They said they wanted to find a windy place with hills and no trees. The Weather Bureau said that Kitty Hawk, North Carolina fit that **description**. It had a long, wide beach. It had sand dunes and no trees. It was windy in the fall.

The brothers also wanted to know what the town was like. William J. Tate told them it had everything they needed. He **invited** them to come and to try out their glider. They went to Kitty Hawk. They chose a remote, sandy area near Kitty Hawk. There, they practiced for four years. Finally, on Dec 17, 1903, they were successful.

A.
1. contacted ___
2. description ___
3. ended up ___
4. goal ___
5. ground ___

    a. something that you hope to do in the future
    b. wrote to or called someone by telephone
    c. the surface of the earth
    d. details of what someone or something is like
    e. came to be in a place not expected

B.
1. invited ___
2. lasted ___
3. location ___
4. moment ___
5. progress ___

    a. a particular point in time
    b. a place
    c. asked somebody to go somewhere
    d. the process of getting better at doing something
    e. continued for a period of time

DISCUSS THE THEME

Read these questions and discuss them with a partner. Share your ideas with the class.

1. The Wright brothers practiced for four years. What problems do you think they had?

2. Why do you think the Wright brothers worked in secret?

CHAPTER 3
THE CONCORDE

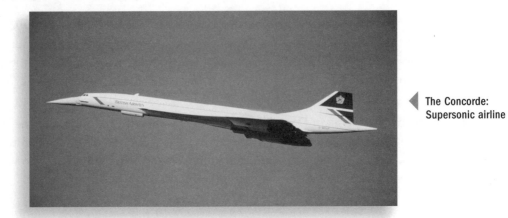

The Concorde: Supersonic airline

PREPARE TO LISTEN

Look at the picture above. Discuss these questions.

1. What do you know about the Concorde?

2. Have you seen one or flown in one? Do you know anyone who has? What was it like?

WORD FOCUS 1

Match the words with their definitions.

alone	jet	speed of sound
fleet	Mach	supersonic

1. a fast type of airplane _____
2. the rate at which sound travels _____
3. a group of planes owned by the same company _____
4. faster than the speed of sound _____
5. without any other company _____
6. a unit for measuring the speed of a plane (in relation to the speed of sound)
   _____

MAKE A PREDICTION

Over 2 million passengers traveled on the Concorde.

a. True   **b.** False

🎧 **Now listen to a museum audio on the Concorde. Check your prediction.**

Listen to the audio again and answer the questions. Circle your answers.

MAIN IDEA

1. What is the main topic?
   A. when the Concorde was developed
   B. who developed the Concorde
   C. what the Concorde was able to do
   D. why the Concorde stopped flying

DETAIL

2. How long did the Concorde fly?
   A. for 12 years
   B. for 17 years
   C. for 21 years
   D. for 27 years

3. Most of the flights were across the Pacific Ocean.
   A. True
   B. False

4. The Concorde was first used for commercial service in
   A. 1967
   B. 1976
   C. 1977
   D. 1979

5. Both British Airways and Air France used the Concorde.
   A. True
   B. False

6. What was the main reason passengers liked the Concorde?
   A. It was interesting to fly in.
   B. It had daily flights.
   C. It took about half the time of a regular airliner.
   D. It flew higher than a regular airliner.

7. The Concorde flew
   A. below the speed of sound
   B. at half the speed of sound
   C. at the speed of sound
   D. at two times the speed of sound

8. It cruised at about
   A. 30,000 feet (about 9,000 meters)
   B. 40,000 feet (about 12,000 meters)
   C. 50,000 feet (about 15,000 meters)
   D. 60,000 feet (about 18,000 meters)

INFERENCE

9. Why did another plane in the sky look like it was flying backwards?
   A. It wasn't as fast.
   B. It wasn't as high.
   C. It wasn't as big.
   D. It wasn't as heavy.

10. Which of the following is true about the Concorde?
    A. It cost a lot of money to fly on it.
    B. It still flies across the Atlantic Ocean.
    C. It never had an accident.
    D. Passengers wanted more daily flights.

Read this student's e-mail about the museum audio. Notice the bold words. Then match the bold words to their definitions below.

> Wow! The Concorde was a supersonic plane. It flew faster than the speed of sound. They brought out the first Concorde in Toulouse, France, on December 11, 1967. That must have been amazing to see. And, how great to work for British Airways or Air France. In 1977, they started **daily** flights between Paris and London, and New York. The Concorde flew for 27 years, from 1976 to 2003. It **transported** more than 2.5 million **passengers**.
>
> I wish I had been able to fly on the Concorde. Passengers liked the Concorde because it was so fast. It flew at two times the speed of sound! A flight between London and New York took about three and a half hours. A **normal** flight takes between seven and eight hours. The **record** for a Concorde flight was under three hours. The Concorde also flew much higher than regular airliners. It **cruised** at about 60,000 feet (about 18,000 meters).
>
> I'd like to see another plane look like it was flying **backwards**. That crash in Paris in 2000 was bad. I understand why Air France **grounded** the Concorde for one year after that. They started flying again in 2001, but there weren't enough passengers. In 2003, they **retired** the Concorde. I'd like to go see one **on display** in a museum.

A.

1. backwards ___   **a.** every day
2. cruised ___   **b.** regular; usual
3. daily ___   **c.** forced an airplane not to fly
4. grounded ___   **d.** in a way that is opposite to the usual
5. normal ___   **e.** traveled, staying at the same speed

B.

1. on display ___   **a.** the best ever
2. passengers ___   **b.** being shown
3. record ___   **c.** people traveling in a vehicle, but not driving
4. retired ___   **d.** moved from one place to another in a vehicle
5. transported ___   **e.** stopped using forever

DISCUSS THE THEME

Read these questions and discuss them with a partner. Share your ideas with the class.

1. Do you think the Concorde should be used again? Why or why not?

2. What do you think the airplane of the future will be like? Give details.

VOCABULARY REVIEW

Fill in the blanks with words from each box.

claimed	controversy	pioneer	retired

1. Alberto Santos-Dumont was considered an aviation _____. He did things no one had done before.

2. The Wright brothers _____ to be the first men to fly an airplane.

3. There was a _____ about the first man to fly. Santos-Dumont flew in public first.

4. Air France and British Airways _____ their fleets of Concordes in 2003.

contact	invited	lasted	steer

5. When the wind shifted direction, the pilot had to _____ the airport. He asked which runway to use.

6. The flight only _____ for a short time, but it made flight history.

7. The people in Kitty Hawk _____ the Wright brothers to come there.

8. It was difficult to _____ an airship in a high wind. It was hard to control it.

WRONG WORD

One word in each group does not fit. Circle the word.

1. transported   cruised   grounded   carried
2. shifted   stopped   remained   stayed
3. mistakes   accomplishments   problems   issues
4. aviation   moment   aircraft   jet
5. captain   crew   passenger   record
6. normal   strange   unusual   odd

WORD FAMILIES

Fill in the blanks with words from each box.

description (*noun*)   descriptive (*adjective*)   describe (*verb*)

1. The letter was very _____. It included a lot of information about the town.
2. The _____ was very good. Kitty Hawk looked just like they expected it to.
3. It wasn't difficult for the man at the weather station to _____ the weather there.

accomplishment (*noun*)   accomplished (*adjective*)   accomplish (*verb*)

4. It was a big _____ to build an airplane that would fly.
5. The Wright brothers worked hard to _____ their goal.
6. Santos-Dumont was an _____ inventor. He was very skilled and successful.

WRAP IT UP

PROJECT WORK

Talk to 2–4 people outside of class about their experiences flying. Ask the following questions and questions of your own:

- Where did you fly? What type of plane was it?
- Did anything interesting or unusual happen on the flight? What did you and the other passengers do?
- What do you like about flying? What do you not like about flying?

Work in small groups. Take turns telling each other what you found out.

INTERNET RESEARCH

Go online and find information about some event in the history of aviation. Find answers to the following questions:

- What is special about this event? When did it happen?
- Which people or countries were involved?
- How did this event affect aviation?

Print a photo, if you can. Present your information to the class.

ESSENTIAL LISTENING SKILLS: ANSWER KEY AND EXPLANATIONS

WHAT TO DO BEFORE YOU LISTEN

A.

1. *Possible answer:* It's a robot. The robot is moving like it's dancing.

2. *Possible answer:* The passage will probably be about robots.

B.

1. *Possible answer:* The passage will be about robots that people have in their homes.

2. *Possible answer:* This kind of robot is called a humanoid robot.

3. Answers will vary.

4. Answers will vary.

> **TIP: Think about what you know about a topic before you listen. As you listen, compare what you hear to what you already know.**

C.

1. Answers will vary.

2. Answers will vary.

> **TIP: Look ahead for any words you may hear before you listen. Then you will be able to recognize these words in the passage.**

D.

True. The passage says there's a huge robot that can vacuum in office buildings.

> **TIP: Read the questions before you listen. Use these to help you know what to listen for.**

WHAT TO DO WHILE YOU LISTEN

E.

1. What is the main topic?

   A is true, but it's not the main topic.

   B may or may not be true, but it's not stated in the passage.

   C is true, but it's not the main topic.

   D is true. This is the main topic.

F.

2. What is planned in Korea and Japan?

   A is not correct. The plans are for every home to have a robot, not for every person to have one.

   B is not correct. The date is 2015, not 2050 and the plans are for every home, not for every person.

   C is correct. In Korea and Japan, there are plans for every home to have a robot by the year 2015.

   D is not correct. The date is 2015, not 2050.

   > **TIP: Listen carefully for numbers, especially the difference between numbers such as 15 and 50.**

3. Robotic toys

   A is not correct. Some robotic toys are pets.

   B is not correct. Robotic toys are made primarily for children.

   C is true. They have sensors that find and recognize different kinds of information.

   D is not correct. Robots respond to people. They do not have feelings and cannot want anything.

   > **TIP: Read the choices carefully.**

4. Which of the following is **not** true?

   A is not the correct answer because it is true. A social robot interacts with people.

   B is not the correct answer because it is true. A social robot has sensors to recognize voices.

   C is the correct answer. A social robot is not designed to do work that people often do, so this statement is not true.

   D is not the correct answer because it is true. A social robot is designed to keep adults company.

   > **TIP: Be careful of a word like *not*.**

5. Almost a million people own robots that clean the floor.

   A is not correct.

   B is correct. The sentence is false because over a million people have already bought these small home robots.

   > **TIP: Listen carefully for words that quantify such as *almost*, *over*, or *more than*.**

6. Robots in office buildings do **not**

   A is incorrect. Robots in office buildings do vacuum.

   B is correct. Robots in office buildings do not write letters.

   C is incorrect. Robots in office buildings do keep watch for fire and robberies.

   D is incorrect. Robots in office buildings do welcome people and answer questions.

7. A humanoid robot is different because it

   A is incorrect. Many robots can talk.

   B is incorrect. Many robots can clean the house.

   C is incorrect. Many robots can respond to people.

   D is correct. Humanoid robots are robots that look like people.

   > **TIP: As you listen, try to picture what you are hearing.**

8. At the moment, humanoid robots

   A is incorrect. Humanoid robots are not used to keep older people company.

   B is incorrect. Humanoid robots cannot do anything that people do.

   C is correct. Humanoid robots cost too much right now to be very common.

   D is incorrect. Humanoid robots are not used to serve people food and drinks in hospitals yet. However, they may be in the future.

   > **TIP: Sometimes you need to listen for details in different sections of the passage.**

G.

9. You have to train a social robot to

   A is incorrect. The robot can move already.

   B is incorrect. The robot can use sensors already.

   C is incorrect. The robot can make sounds already.

   D is correct. You have to teach the robot to recognize your voice commands.

   > **TIP: Eliminate any choices that you know are wrong.**

10. In the future, which of these will probably be true?

    A is incorrect. Some robots are too big now. In the future they will probably be smaller, not bigger.

    B is correct. Robots are too expensive now. In the future they will probably be less expensive.

    C is incorrect. Robots of the future may look more human, but they still won't have feelings.

    D is incorrect. All of the above must be correct for this to be the correct answer.

    > **TIP: Don't choose the first answer that is correct. Read all of the choices.**

H.

1. **B** They <u>move and make noises when you touch them</u>, so they seem to **respond** to you.

2. **C** They are making **social** robots for adults, <u>especially for older people who may not be able to get out and see other people a lot</u>.

3. **B** These robots **interact** with their owners and <u>keep them company</u>.

4. They can do this because they have **sensors** that <u>find and recognize different kinds of information</u>.

5. You give it a **command**. For example, you can tell it to <u>clean the floor</u>.

6. But the most interesting robots are **humanoid** robots—<u>robots that look like people</u>.

VOCABULARY INDEX

COMMON IRREGULAR VERBS

INFINITIVE	SIMPLE PAST	PAST PARTICIPLE	INFINITIVE	SIMPLE PAST	PAST PARTICIPLE
be	was/were	been	let	let	let
become	became	become	light	lit/lighted	lit/lighted
begin	began	begun	lose	lost	lost
blow	blew	blown	make	made	made
break	broke	broken	mean	meant	meant
bring	brought	brought	meet	met	met
build	built	built	pay	paid	paid
buy	bought	bought	put	put	put
catch	caught	caught	read	read	read
choose	chose	chosen	ride	rode	ridden
come	came	come	ring	rang	rung
cost	cost	cost	run	ran	run
cut	cut	cut	say	said	said
do	did	done	see	saw	seen
draw	drew	drawn	sell	sold	sold
drive	drove	driven	send	sent	sent
eat	ate	eaten	set	set	set
fall	fell	fallen	show	showed	shown
feel	felt	felt	sing	sang	sung
find	found	found	sit	sat	sat
fly	flew	flown	sleep	slept	slept
forget	forgot	forgotten	speak	spoke	spoken
freeze	froze	frozen	spend	spent	spent
get	got	gotten	stand	stood	stood
give	gave	given	steal	stole	stolen
go	went	gone/been	swim	swam	swum
grow	grew	grown	take	took	taken
hang	hung	hung	teach	taught	taught
have	had	had	tear	tore	torn
hear	heard	heard	tell	told	told
hold	held	held	think	thought	thought
hurt	hurt	hurt	throw	threw	thrown
keep	kept	kept	understand	understood	understood
know	knew	known	wear	wore	worn
lay	laid	laid	win	won	won
leave	left	left	write	wrote	written